The Vocabul-

Also by David Hastings

Over the Mountains of the Sea
Extra! Extra! How the people made the news
The Many Deaths of Mary Dobie
Odyssey of the Unknown Anzac

The Vocabulary Detective

*How to get meaning from context.
A guide for English learners*

David Hastings

DMH Press

First published 2022
DMH Press
Auckland
New Zealand
dmhcosmo@outlook.com

© 2022 David Hastings
All rights reserved

ISBN: 9798771411583

This book is copyright. Apart from fair dealing for the purpose of private study, research, criticism or review, no part may be reproduced by any process without prior permission of the publisher. The moral rights of the author have been asserted.

Cover design: Micaela Hastings, www.mhastingsdesign.com
Cover image: iStock/and2DesignInc

Table of Contents

Introduction 1

The Vocabulary Detective's Guide ... 5

A Sincere Apology 13

Champagne Charlie 25

The Lucky Number Fourteen.......... 43

My Favourite Photo 63

Devil in the Detail 87

The Buffalo's Dilemma 99

About the author 123

Introduction

The idea for this book came from a discussion in an advanced English class at the NZLC language school in Auckland, New Zealand. The topic was the importance of reading for pleasure to expand your vocabulary, especially reading authentic texts. The point was that you would be more likely to learn from an interesting subject than a boring one.

All the students agreed that it was a very good idea but there was one big problem. Even at advanced level they found there were so many unfamiliar words and expressions in authentic texts that they had to stop numerous times on every page to look up the dictionary. As a result, reading became a pain instead of a pleasure and the learning potential was lost.

Fortunately there was one student in the class who spoke up and said it was a big mistake to reach for the dictionary whenever you saw a word you didn't know. It was much better, he said, to keep reading and to try to work out the meaning for yourself from the context.

The students listened to him not just because he was the best speaker in the class but also because English was his fifth language. He already spoke French, German, Italian and Greek so it seemed clear that he knew what he was talking about when it came to learning languages.

There is no doubt that his advice was good. If you listen to language teachers or experienced language learners, they nearly

The Vocabulary Detective

always say that working out the meaning from the context is a much better way of expanding your vocabulary that relying only on a dictionary.

The aim of this book is to help you to develop the skill of using the context to infer or guess the meaning of words. The good news is that it is not as difficult as it sounds. Any text on any subject is full of synonyms, comparisons, contrasts, details and examples that are valuable clues to the meaning of words you don't know. Sometimes writers even make it especially easy for you by providing definitions.

But the big question is *how* do you do it? How do you recognize the clues? Textbooks sometimes give tips but they usually treat it as a minor skill whereas I think it deserves much greater emphasis. You should become a vocabulary detective. That is, you need to treat unknown words or expressions as mysteries to be solved, just like a detective solves crimes. But to do this you need to know the right questions to ask yourself and learn to recognize the clues.

The next section of this book is a detailed guide which explains the process.

After the guide there are six entertaining short stories with selected words and expressions to help you practice. Each story is followed by notes for vocabulary detectives which show the questions to ask and the clues to notice for each of the selected words and expressions. Your task is to use them to work out the meanings for yourself before checking the dictionary.

The stories are suitable for intermediate to advanced students. The Text Inspector website grades them all at B1 level for reading under the Common European Framework of Reference for languages (CEFR), so intermediate students should be able to understand the context. However, the stories are all written in authentic English and contain many words that

Introduction

Text Inspector grades at C1 and C2 plus many colloquial and idiomatic expressions.

It is likely that you will know some of the selected words but you should not forget that the main point of this book is not just to teach new vocabulary but to help you develop your skills as a vocabulary detective. You should practice the skill even if you already know the highlighted words.

Perhaps the most important benefit of learning vocabulary like this is that you get a sense of how words are used in different ways and with different meanings when they appear in different contexts. But it should also reduce the number of times you have to look up words in the dictionary and therefore make reading more enjoyable and more effective in expanding your vocabulary.

There are two other points worth bearing in mind. The first is that vocabulary detectives, just like real detectives, do not always manage to solve the mystery. Sometimes you will misinterpret the clues and get the meaning wrong. And sometimes you will not be able to find any clues at all so you won't even be able to make a guess.

The second important point to bear in mind is that working out the meaning from context, though extremely useful, is not enough by itself to learn a language. It is one thing to know the meaning of a word or expression, quite another to be able to use it. So, as always, you need to keep practicing the major skills of the language: listening, speaking and writing as well as reading for pleasure.

The vocabulary detective's guide

The most important rule of being a good vocabulary detective is to understand the context before you start asking questions and looking for clues.

The basic way to do this is to follow the simple three-step process that is used in most reading or listening activities in ESL classrooms.

First, you look at the title and maybe the first two or three paragraphs and try to predict what the story is about. Then you read the whole story for gist, or general meaning, and when you have finished check your understanding against your prediction. Do not stop to look up words in the dictionary at this stage.

Next you read it again more carefully to get a more detailed understanding of the context. Ask yourself simple wh-questions to help you focus on the details and check your understanding:

Who is this story about?
What happens in the story?
When do things happen?
Where do they happen?
Why do they happen?
How do they happen?

The context will give you the general idea such as whether the text is formal or informal, serious or humorous, fiction or non-fiction, positive or negative, ironic or literal.

When you have completed the three-step reading process and understand the context, you will be ready to start working out the specific meaning of any words and expressions you don't know.

For the purposes of this book, certain words and expressions in each story have been highlighted in bold and analysed in the "Clues in the Context" notes that follow each story. These are there to give you guided practice.

You begin by asking simple questions that will help you to find the clues. When you have found the clues you will notice what type of clues they are and, finally, you will use the clues to work out the meaning.

Below you will find the basic questions numbered 1-5. After that, the clue types are defined A-F. These numbers and letters are used in the notes so you can relate the questions and clues back to this guide.

The Questions

1. What part of speech is it? Is it a noun, a verb, an adjective or an adverb?

This question is important because once you answer it you can ask a series of follow-up questions that should lead to you the clues. It is surprising how often the meaning of the word occurs to learners once they identify the part of speech.

2. If it's a noun ask: Who or what is it?

To answer this question you have to search the text for a clue. For example look at the noun **thug** in the Clues in the Context notes on the first story, *A Sincere Apology* (page 22). If you ask yourself "who or what is it?" You will soon find the answer.

3. If it's a verb ask: What action or state does it express? And who or what does it refer to?

For an example look at the verb "alternating" in *A Sincere Apology* (p. 18).

4. If it is an adverb or adjective ask: What does it describe? What word does it qualify and how does it modify the meaning? Does it make the word stronger or weaker? Is it positive or negative?

For example look at "grudging" in the notes on *A Sincere Apology* (p.22).

5. Is it an idiom?

An idiom is a group of words that we treat as a single unit of language. It is really important to recognise idioms because you usually cannot work out the meaning by looking at each word separately. Idioms include multi-word verbs, collocations and colloquial expressions. They also include chunks of language which are set or prefabricated ways of saying things. For idioms you ask the same questions you would ask for nouns, verbs and adjectives.

For multi-word verbs ask the same question you would ask for any verb: What action or state does it express? And who or what does it refer to? See, for example "pacing up and down" in *A Sincere Apology* (p. 21).

Collocations are usually combinations of adjectives and nouns so start by asking what the noun is and then follow up by asking yourself how the adjective modifies its meaning. For example "premature labor" in *A Sincere Apology* (p. 17).

Colloquial expressions can be much more difficult at first because often the words do not relate directly to the meaning. For instance the expression "to let sleeping dogs lie" in *A*

Sincere Apology (p. 22) has got nothing to do with sleeping or dogs. To find the meaning you should first identify the key word in the expression and then ask the appropriate question. In this case it is the verb "to let" so you should ask what action or state it expresses and who or what does it refer to. For the clues check the notes.

The clues

Below are six different types of clue that you should learn to recognise and use. They are: clues in the word itself, synonyms, details and specific examples, definitions, comparisons and contrasts and, finally, clues that occur in different contexts.

A. The word itself

Before you start looking at the context, look closely at the word itself.

For instance, the adverb "icily" appears in *The Lucky Number Fourteen* (p. 55). One way to work out the meaning is to ask yourself if there is another form of the word – a noun, verb or adjective – that you already know and therefore might reveal the meaning of "icily".

Prefixes are also useful clues if you know the base word. For instance, the prefix "post" in "postscript" which appears at the end of *A Sincere Apology* (p. 24).

Sometimes a word is made by joining two other words together. If you know what one or the other means, it will help you work out the meaning of the combined word. For example "teamwork" in *The Lucky Number Fourteen* (p. 58).

B. Synonyms

After you have looked closely at the word itself, you can start searching the context for clues. Every piece of writing contains certain ideas and themes that are repeated in different ways to make the meaning clear or to emphasise certain points. If you learn to recognise these repetitions it will help you to unlock the meanings of words you don't know.

Among the most common clues, and the easiest to recognise and use, are synonyms. Writers who need to repeat ideas but want to avoid repeating the same word over and over again will often use synonyms. Sometimes they do this for emphasis and clarity as well.

An example of the first type of synonym, is the word "essence" in the notes on *Champagne Charlie* (p. 37). The writer repeats the idea in the next sentence with a phrase that, in the context, means more or less the same as "essence".

Sometimes writers will give a range of synonyms for emphasis and clarity. For instance the expression "a cut above the rest" in *My Favourite Photo* is accompanied by a series of similar expressions (p. 71). It is well worth noting this example because, especially when speaking, people will often mention a series of similar words before settling on the one that best expresses what they want to say.

And, on this point, you might have noticed that the words "infer" and "guess" and the multi-word verb "work out the meaning of" used in the introduction to this book, are very similar. So if you know only one of them, you should be able to work out the meaning of the other two.

C. Definitions

Writers sometimes help their readers by giving definitions. Clues like this are very easy to understand but they are not nearly as common as synonyms. Usually definitions appear when a word is unusual or has a very specific meaning that the writer wants to convey. Although definitions are not common, you should watch out for them. They are like having a dictionary embedded in the text!

For example, see the word "dilemma" defined by the character of the professor in *The Buffalo's Dilemma* (p.111).

D. Examples and specific details

These clues are the most common. Writers often give examples or specific details of what they are referring to. These are not as easy to use as synonyms or definitions but it is worth the effort because you can work back from the details and examples to make a pretty good guess.

For instance, from the details in *A Sincere Apology*, you should be able to work out the meaning of "staining" (p. 19).

E. Comparisons and contrasts

Writers sometimes emphasise and clarify what they mean by drawing comparisons and contrasts and in this way provide valuable clues for vocabulary detectives.

For an example of a comparison, look at the adjective "stern" in *Devil in the Detail* (p. 97). It is used to describe a newspaper editor and to clarify the meaning, he is compared to a strict schoolteacher.

For an example of a contrast, look at the expression "struggling to make ends meet" in *Champagne Charlie* (p. 32). It is used to contrast Charlie with Evelyn Somerset who was "very, very rich".

F. Same words, different context

Seeing the same word or expression in different contexts is important for four reasons.

The most obvious one is that if you could not work out the meaning the first time you saw it, this gives you another chance.

Second, if you did work out the meaning, seeing it again is a way of checking your understanding.

Third, if you've seen the word before but cannot remember what it means, look for fresh clues. You'll find it much easier the next time. Indeed, repetition is essential to learning vocabulary. Hardly anyone ever learned a word just by looking at it once.

And fourth, and most importantly, you will see how the word can change its meaning in different contexts. For example, the word "dull" in *My Favourite Photo* is used in two different senses and the only way to tell the difference is by relating the word to its context (pp. 75, 84).

Notes for vocabulary detectives

At the end of each story are the notes for vocabulary detectives which highlight the questions and clues for each of the words and expressions in bold. They are followed by the relevant quotation from the story with the clues underlined. All you have to do is infer, guess or work out the meaning.

Next steps

Only when you have done your detective work should you consult a dictionary and preferably you should do this only to check your understanding.

A more valuable exercise is to do a lot of listening and reading and try to notice this vocabulary in other contexts.

And, of course, you should practice your vocabulary detective skills on other texts with other unfamiliar words and expressions.

And finally ... use it!

The most important part of all is to practice using new vocabulary in writing or speaking. So try writing sentences using your new words but, above all, use them in speaking practice in class or with your language buddies.

A Sincere Apology

Ring, ring. Ring, ring. Ring, ring. In the old days phones used to ring like that. This particular phone was on the bedside table of Dr. John Bell and it was ringing at two o'clock in the morning.

Old Dr. Bell was used to being **woken up** like this. Whenever there was an emergency, the hospital would call him. He was their most experienced surgeon and always knew what to do.

Ring, ring. He usually tried to answer the phone after just three rings, no matter what time of night it was. But this morning it was just too hard. He had been in a deep sleep when the phone suddenly **woke him up**.

Ring, ring. He let it ring one more time and then he picked up the receiver and answered it.

"Hello."

On the other end of the phone was the duty nurse from the maternity ward who told him that Mrs. Harper had gone into **premature labor** and he was needed urgently.

"Okay, I'll be right there," said the old doctor even though he didn't really feel like it. It was cold and it was raining heavily outside. All he really wanted to do was to roll over in his warm, soft bed and go straight back to sleep. But he knew his duty and when a woman was about to give birth sooner than expected, his duty was to be at her bedside.

The Vocabulary Detective

"I'm getting too old for this," he muttered to himself as he switched on his bedside light. His wife did not stir as he got dressed. She was as used to the early morning emergencies as he was. It was a normal part of their life together.

He shut the door quietly as he went out and then drove to the hospital through the heavy rain. Slip, slap. Slip, slap. Slip, slap went the windscreen wipers. They were going as fast as they could but the rain was so heavy that no sooner had they wiped the water off the windscreen than it was back again. So he drove the whole way **alternating** between blurred visibility and clear visibility. Slip, slap. Slip, slap. Slip, slap.

It was in a moment of blurred visibility when he turned into the hospital car park and he didn't notice a car coming from the opposite direction. The two cars turned into the hospital at exactly the same time.

Crash! They collided at the entrance. There was no serious damage, both cars had been travelling very slowly because of the rain. But the other car was blocking the doctor's way into the hospital.

The driver of the other car got out. He was a big man. Tall and thick-set and he ignored the rain as he walked directly to the doctor's car.

Old Dr. Bell wound down his window. He was going to tell the man that he was a doctor on his way to an emergency and therefore should go first. But before he could say anything, the big man **swung his fist** and punched him in the face.

Dr. Bell was knocked back into his seat with blood **pouring out** of his nose and the rain **pouring in** through the open window. He was shocked and shaken. He knew that his nose was broken and the blood was **staining** his white shirt red. Meanwhile, the big man turned, went back to his car, **revved the engine** and drove through the gates.

Dr. Bell took a few moments to pull himself together and by the time he parked near the hospital's main entrance, there was no sign of the big man or his car.

The old doctor cleaned himself up as best he could but when he entered the delivery suite the nurses were shocked by his appearance. By now his nose had swelled up and he had a black eye.

"What happened to you?" asked the senior nurse.

"I was punched on the nose in a **road-rage** incident," replied Dr. Bell and he quickly told her the story before they got down to work to help Mrs. Harper give birth to her first baby who turned out to be a healthy baby boy even though he was born a little **prematurely**.

With the emergency over, Dr. Bell went to break the happy news to the father who, as usual in those days, was **pacing up and down** anxiously from one side of the waiting room to the other.

Dr. Bell recognized him instantly. There was no mistaking the big man who had punched him in the face and broken his nose just a couple of hours before.

It was obvious the big man recognized Dr. Bell too. What should have been the happiest moment of his life was spoiled by his deep embarrassment. Of course he had no choice but to apologize. He struggled to make eye contact. He looked at the floor and finally, he muttered a few words of **grudging** apology which Dr. Bell could hardly hear. However, the doctor accepted the apology, shook the man's hand and left him to join his wife and his new-born son.

It was dawn when the old doctor got home, sore and bloody. His nose was swollen and red and his black eye was a real "shiner". And his shirt was ruined.

"What on earth happened to you," said his wife when she saw him. And the old doctor told the story.

"What a **thug**! What a brute! What a violent man!" said the doctor's wife, "I hope you're going to report him to the police."

"No, certainly not," said old Dr. Bell. "He was pretty stressed and, in any case, he said sorry."

"Well, I don't think that's good enough," she said. "Look, he's not only ruined you nice new shirt but he's given you a broken nose and a black eye as well."

"I know, I know," said Dr. Bell who was really tired by now. He had had a long, difficult night. "It won't help matters to call the police. I'm sure he really regrets it and involving the police will only make it worse for him."

In the end, they agreed to disagree. She insisted the man's apology was not enough and that her husband should report him to the police. Her husband wanted **to let sleeping dogs lie**. A bad thing had happened, but now it was finished and there was no point creating more trouble for everyone.

The tension eased in the afternoon when a parcel was delivered to the Bells' house. Inside was a new white shirt and a bottle of Scotch whisky. There was also a note which read: "I am sorry for what I did last night. It should have been the happiest moment in my life but I spoiled it by my violent behavior and made the whole thing worse with my **surly and churlish** apology to you. However, it is obvious to me now, as it should have been then, that nothing short of a sincere apology will do. So can I just say I'm sorry and that I hope you will accept these gifts as a **token** or sign of my sincerity?"

It was a handsome apology: full, frank and sincere and more than enough to satisfy the doctor's wife. But what made it even sweeter was the **postscript**, the few words added at the end: "PS we're calling him John".

A Sincere Apology

Clues in the Context

Woken up / woke him up

(5) An idiom which is a multi-word verb, so ask yourself: What state or action does it express? And who does it refer to?

(D) Obviously it refers to Dr. Bell and the clue is the specific detail in the story that tells you what he was doing before the phone rang.

> Old Dr. Bell was used to being **woken up** like this. Whenever there was an emergency, the hospital would call him. He was their most experienced surgeon and always knew what to do.
>
> Ring, ring. He usually tried to answer the phone after just three rings, no matter what time of night it was. But this morning it was just too hard. <u>He had been in a deep sleep</u> when the phone suddenly **woke him up**.

So what do you think it means?

Premature labor

(5) This is an idiom or collocation made up of an adjective and a noun. So you should ask: What is "labor" and how does the adjective "premature" modify its meaning? There are three clues.

(A) First, look closely at the adjective and note that it has the prefix "pre" meaning before. This is a clue to what was particular or special about this woman's labor.

(C) The best clue comes in the following paragraph where the idea is repeated, this time as a definition.

(D) And finally, the detail that tells you Mrs. Harper was in the maternity ward is also a good clue. If you can answer the question "why was she in the maternity ward?" you will be getting close to the meaning.

> On the other end of the phone was the duty nurse from the <u>maternity ward</u> who told him that Mrs. Harper had gone into **premature labor** and he was needed urgently.

"Okay, I'll be right there," said the old doctor even though he didn't really feel like it. It was cold and it was raining heavily outside. All he really wanted to do was to roll over in his warm, soft bed and go straight back to sleep. But he knew his duty and when a woman was about <u>to give birth sooner than expected</u>, his duty was to be at her bedside.

Meaning...

Alternating

(3) This is a verb expressing an action so ask: What is happening? What does it refer to?

(D) The answers are the specific details that immediately follow to tell you that one moment he could see clearly and the next moment he couldn't.

> They were going as fast as they could but the rain was so heavy that no sooner had they wiped the water off the windscreen than it was back again. So he drove the whole way **alternating** between <u>blurred visibility</u> and <u>clear visibility</u>.

Meaning...

A Sincere Apology

Swung his fist

(5) This is an idiom, a colloquial expression made up of the verb "swung" and the noun "fist". So ask first "what is a fist?" And second, "what action is expressed here and who does it refer to?"

(D) The clue is in the specific detail that follows which should give you a good idea of what was meant by "swung his fist".

> But before he could say anything, the big man **swung his fist** and punched him in the face.

Meaning...

Pouring out / pouring in

(5) Two multi-word verbs. So ask: what action do they express and what do they refer to.

(D) The specific details of the story give you the clues that should help you imagine the scene and therefore understand the meaning. The first one refers to blood and his nose, the second to the rain and the open window of the car.

> Dr. Bell was knocked back into his seat with blood **pouring out** of his nose and the rain **pouring in** through the open window. He was shocked and shaken.

Meaning of pouring out...
Meaning of pouring in...

Staining

(3) A verb, so ask: What action does it express? And what does it refer to?

The Vocabulary Detective

(D) The clues are to be found in specific details. The sentence makes it clear that his shirt was changing color and this was caused by the blood coming from his nose.

> He knew that his nose was broken and the <u>blood</u> was **staining** his <u>white shirt red</u>.

Meaning…

Revved the engine

(5) This is a colloquial expression made up of a verb and a noun. Ask yourself about the noun first: What is it? When you have the answer ask about the verb: What action does it express?

(D) This question directs you to the detail that follows which should give you a clue to the meaning of "revved the engine".

> Meanwhile, the big man turned, went back to his car, **revved the engine** and <u>drove through the gates</u>.

Meaning…

Road-rage

(4) Adjective so ask: What word does it qualify and in what way?

(D) The answer to the first question is that it qualifies the word "incident". It tells you what kind of incident it was but to get the precise meaning you need to look back at the story for the details of how there was a minor car crash which resulted in an angry man assaulting another man.

A Sincere Apology

"I was punched on the nose in a **road-rage** incident," replied Dr. Bell…

Meaning…

Prematurely
(F) The adverb form of the adjective "premature" which you have already seen. The context is slightly different, this time it refers to the birth of the child rather than the labor of the woman. But the meaning is essentially the same.

> Mrs. Harper give birth to her first baby who turned out to be a healthy baby boy even though he was born a little **prematurely**.

Meaning…

Pacing up and down
(5) A verbal idiom so ask: What action does it express and who is performing the action?
(D) The answer to the second question is obvious, it is something that the father is doing. The answer to the first question gives you the specific detail which should help you to work out what "pacing up and down" means.

> With the emergency over, Dr. Bell went to break the happy news to the father who, as usual in those days, was **pacing up and down** anxiously from one side of the waiting room to the other.

Meaning…

The Vocabulary Detective

Grudging

(4) An adjective so ask: What word does it qualify and how does it modify the meaning? Does it make the word stronger or weaker, negative or positive?

(D) "Grudging" qualifies the noun "apology" which you should know. The clues are in the details describing the way the man makes the apology. These details will help you work out whether the adjective is positive or negative.

> <u>He struggled to make eye contact</u>. <u>He looked at the floor</u> and finally, <u>he muttered</u> a few words of **grudging** apology which Dr. Bell could hardly hear.

Meaning...

Thug

(2) A noun, so ask: What is it? There are two clues.

(B) The first clues is a synonym "brute".

(C) The second clue is a definition "a violent man".

> "What a **thug**! What a <u>brute</u>! What a <u>violent man</u>!" said the doctor's wife.

Meaning...

To let sleeping dogs lie

(5) A colloquial expression that has nothing to do with sleeping dogs. However, it begins with a verb "to let" so ask: What state was the husband expressing?

(D) The clue is in the specific detail in the next sentence.

> Her husband wanted **to let sleeping dogs lie**. A bad thing had happened, but now <u>it was</u>

<u>finished and there was no point creating more trouble for everyone</u>.

Meaning…

Surly and churlish

(5) Two adjectives often used together as a collocation. So ask: What noun do they qualify and how do they modify its meaning? Do they make the noun stronger or weaker, positive or negative?

(E) The modified noun is "apology" and the clue to understanding the meaning of the two adjectives is in the contrasting adjective used in the next sentence: "sincere" which modifies "apology" in a different way. Using this contrast you should be able to work out the meaning of "surly and churlish" and whether these are positive or negative words.

(F) You could also note that the "apology" appears above with the adjective "grudging" which should help you to check your understanding and clarify the meaning of "surly and churlish".

> There was also a note which read: "I am sorry for what I did the last night. It should have been the happiest moment in my life but I spoiled it by my violent behavior and made the whole thing worse with my **surly and churlish** apology to you. However, it is obvious to me now, as it should have been then, that nothing short of a <u>sincere</u> apology will do."

Meaning…

Token

(2) A noun, so ask: What is it?

(B) The answer follows immediately. It is a synonym signaled by "or". In other words the writer is giving an alternative word to express the same meaning.

> So can I just say I'm sorry and that I hope you will accept these gifts as a **token** or sign of my sincerity?"

Meaning...

Postscript

(2) A noun so ask: What is it? There are three clues.

(A) The first clue comes from the word itself. The prefix "post" means "after" and the base word "script" means "writing".

(C) The second clue is a definition.

(D) And the third clue is a specific example of a "postscript".

> But what made it even sweeter was the **postscript**, the few words added at the end: "PS we're calling him John".

Meaning...

Champagne Charlie

One of the juiciest pieces of gossip I ever heard was about how a young man I knew had a wild affair with a famous Hollywood star. I cannot tell you their real names because I don't want to cause any embarrassment so I'll give them pseudonyms. Let's call the young man Charlie Stokes and the star Evelyn Somerset.

Somerset came to our town **at the height of her fame**. She had just starred in a hugely successful movie and had scooped about every acting prize there was. She had star power to burn. She was talented, glamorous, sexy and very, very rich.

Young Charlie, however, was none of those things. He didn't have any special talent or skill that I knew of. He wasn't good looking and he wasn't stylish. I don't think anyone in their wildest dreams would think of him as sexy and he certainly wasn't rich. In fact, **he was struggling to make ends meet.**

So I was a little surprised during a dinner party one night when I first heard hints of **a juicy story** about Charlie and the Hollywood star. Nobody said it directly but they all **implied** that he and Evelyn had had a love affair during her visit a few weeks before. It seemed that no one really knew what the true story was but that didn't stop them filling in the gaps with their imaginations.

Some of us were **skeptical** and expressed doubt about the story. "But what did she see in him?" someone asked. It was a good question. It was not hard to understand what *he* saw in her, but what *she* saw in him was altogether different. For the reasons mentioned above, they were a most **unlikely couple** and the best that anyone could do to answer the question of what she saw in him was the old saying "opposites attract".

I'm a naturally **skeptical** person and I left the dinner party that night thinking that **something didn't add up**. I thought it must have been a rumor. But a few weeks later I met my friends again and they said they had confirmed the story.

"Yes, it's all true," said Tony Ballantyne. "My brother knows someone whose cousin works with the public relations company that handled her visit here. Flowers, champagne, the lot."

As Tony told it, the pair had met at a party given for her after she had appeared on a late night TV chat show. It seemed they had **hit it off instantly**, you might even say it was love at first sight and their first date was a weekend away at a very expensive country resort. She paid, of course, there was no way he could afford to stay in a place like that. They drank champagne and he bought her flowers. Tony claimed his source was reliable and he had all the facts. He claimed that nothing of what he said was **speculation** or rumor, it was all true.

It sounded believable the way Tony told it and it was a great piece of gossip to entertain your friends. But I still couldn't help thinking there was **something that didn't quite add up**. It seemed so unlikely. Of course that was what made the gossip especially **juicy**.

Over the next few weeks I kept hearing the story told again and again by different people. Often the details were different. One version said they had stayed at a well-known winery for the weekend, another said they had gone to the mountains for a spot of skiing. Someone else told us she had personally seen them walking hand-in-hand along a famous beach at sunset, just near one of the most exclusive and expensive resorts in the country.

But these differences were mere details and did not affect the overall story. The **essence** always remained the same. The basic details were that they had met at a party, it was love at first sight, they had drunk Champagne and he had bought her flowers.

Still, there remained **a lot of things that didn't add up** so when I bumped into Charlie himself at a city bar one Friday night I couldn't wait to get the true story right **from the horse's mouth**.

"What's this I hear about you and Evelyn Somerset?" I said, expecting to get the **brush off**, to be told to mind my own business. But, to my surprise, Charlie responded with a big grin and began to talk freely.

"Oh, that," he said. "Wow! That was a great adventure!"

"I bet it was," I said. "Do tell. What happened? All the **juicy** details please!"

The background to the story was that the star had told the organizers of her tour that she wanted to meet some ordinary people. So they got in touch with a guy called Jerry Aitken who was famous for organizing parties. He was only too happy to arrange a party for her.

Charlie was one of the "ordinary people" lucky enough to be invited and he was there when she made her grand entrance.

"I was in the kitchen at the time," said Charlie, "just getting myself another beer. She swept into the house as though she was a queen. She was accompanied by two heavy looking guys, one of whom came into the kitchen with a big white cardboard box.

"He put it carefully on the kitchen table and opened it to reveal a great big bunch of beautiful red roses. But that wasn't all. He lifted the roses out of the box and underneath were two glistening bottles of very expensive Champagne.

"Before I had time to speak, he took one of the bottles and passed it to me with an order: 'open it,' he said as though I was some kind of servant. I did not like the way he spoke to me. I did not like it at all but instead of saying anything back to him, I just took the bottle and began to shake it vigorously.

"He snatched it out of my hands and said 'don't be an idiot.' He put the bottle down on the kitchen table and picked up the other one which he opened himself. The cork came out with a satisfying pop and he poured a fizzing glass to take to his mistress who, by now, was in the sitting room surrounded by her adoring fans.

"When I joined them, the man who had come into the kitchen was standing on Evelyn's right hand side ready to top up the champagne glass which she was sipping from time to time. The other guy was standing on her left holding a little yellow box which looked like a medicine box. It contained a number of glass vials wrapped in **gauze** or light cloth.

"With the champagne in her right hand, she reached into the box with her left hand, took out one of the vials, broke it open, held it up to her nose and **sniffed** it. 'Ahhhh,' she said and then offered the vial to the ordinary men and women surrounding her, each of whom also **sniffed** it. 'Great', 'Wow', 'Fantastic', 'Hey, man' was about all they could say.

"When it was my turn she told me to take **a sniff**, which I did, inhaling the fumes up through my nose. It jolted me. I felt a rush of euphoria and my heart tighten as though it had been squeezed like a ball before being released and bouncing back into shape. There followed a moment of dizziness and I felt as though I was flying and a little bit out of control. Then the feeling ended as quickly as it had started.

"I asked the man standing next to me what these things were and he told me they were 'poppers', the party drug of the day which was really some kind of medicine used to **revive** people having heart attacks. One **sniff** was supposed to bring anyone back to life. 'Great, isn't it?' he said. But, no, I didn't think so.

"I thought it was risky and stupid so I decided to leave the party through the back door. On my way through the kitchen I noticed the flowers and the shaken bottle of very expensive Champagne still sitting on the table. The glistening bottle seemed to be saying 'drink me'.

"I didn't have much use for a big bunch of red roses so I left that behind for Evelyn, but I thought it best to take the Champagne with me. It had to be drunk but one bottle would be more than enough for Evelyn, especially with all those poppers she was **snorting**.

"So I slipped the champagne under my coat and went out into the street where I caught a cab that took me to a flat shared by my mates Jeremy Evans and Mike Horwood. When I arrived they were sitting around the kitchen table feeling slightly bored. 'Hey fellas,' I said, 'look what I got!' and I showed them the bottle. 'By crikey,' said Mike, 'that's the real thing. I've never had French Champagne before!' And Jeremy wanted to know where I'd got it from. 'Let's just say it's a gift from a Hollywood star in appreciation of all I've done for her,' I said.

"Then I told the story of how I had got it. And, of course, they didn't need to be asked twice if they wanted to try it. They had no champagne glasses but they washed out three coffee cups. Then I began the process of opening the bottle. I did it cautiously, mindful of the shaking it had received only an hour or so previously.

"First I tore off the wrapping around the cork. Then I unscrewed the wire cage that held the cork in place. Finally, with the bottle pointed away from my mates, I eased the cork out with my thumbs. It came slowly at first, then it exploded out of the bottle like a cannon shot followed by a spume of froth and sparkle.

"It seemed as though half of the bottle's contents had sprayed across the kitchen before I had time to pour, but even so there was plenty to go around. We raised our coffee mugs to Evelyn Somerset, star of the big screen, and all declared that champagne was the best bloody drink we'd ever had."

So that was Charlie's story. Not what the rumour mill said at all. I looked at him in amazement. "You mean, you didn't have a wild affair with Evelyn Somerset?" I said, and I couldn't hide my disappointment.

"No," he replied. "Where did you ever get that idea?"

"The whole town's talking about it," I said.

"Ha, ha, ha," he laughed, "I wish. But the fact is, the closest I got to her was when she passed me that stuff to sniff. But I must say, that champagne was really good. Nectar of the gods, nectar of the gods," he said raising a **humble** glass of beer to his lips. "So that's it. That's the story of me and Evelyn Somerset. A brief encounter, plenty of champagne and roses but no wild romance. Still, it wasn't a bad story, eh?"

"No," I said, looking at him for a moment in disbelief and reflecting that the old saying about truth being stranger than fiction was not always right. "It's not a bad story. Not bad at all. But to be honest with you, I much preferred the other one."

Clues in the Context

One of the juiciest pieces of gossip

(5) This is an idiomatic expression. It is comprised of a noun "gossip" and a superlative "juiciest" which comes from the adjective "juicy". So ask the standard questions about nouns and adjectives. What is "gossip"? And in what way does "juiciest" modify the meaning? Does it make the meaning stronger or weaker?

(D) These questions should lead you to the clue which gives a specific example of "gossip". The same clue should give you an idea of how "juiciest" modifies the meaning.

> One of the **juiciest pieces of gossip** I ever heard was about how a young man I knew had <u>a wild affair with a famous Hollywood star</u>.

So what do you think it means?

Pseudonyms

(2) A plural noun, so ask: What are they?

(A) Before you look at the context look at the word itself which is made up of two parts. You might recognize "pseudo" which an adjective meaning "fake" of "false"

(E) Now look at the context and you will find the clue at the beginning of the sentence. A contrast is drawn between their real names and the names used in the story. With this clue, and knowing the "pseudo" means false, you should be able to work out the meaning of the word "pseudonym".

> I cannot tell you their <u>real names</u> because I don't want to cause any embarrassment so I'll give them **pseudonyms**.

Meaning…

The Vocabulary Detective

At the height of her fame

(5) This is an idiom that tells you something about Evelyn Somerset. So ask: What was so special about her at that time?

(D) The question points you to the specific details.

> Somerset came to our town **at the height of her fame**. She had just <u>starred in a hugely successful movie</u> and had <u>scooped about every acting prize</u> there was.

Meaning…

He was struggling to make ends meet

(5) An idiom used to describe Charlie. So what does it say about him? This question points to two different clues.

(B) One clue is that "struggling to make ends meet" is a synonym for "he certainly wasn't rich". The idea has been repeated using different words for emphasis and clarity.

(E) The other is that "struggling to make ends meet" is part of a paragraph in which Charlie is contrasted with Evelyn. He is the opposite of her in everything. And she is described as "very, very rich". It follows, therefore, that "struggling to make ends meet" is the opposite of being very rich.

> She was talented, glamorous, sexy and <u>very, very rich</u>.
>
> Young Charlie, however, was none of those things. He didn't have any special talent or skill that I knew of. He wasn't good looking and he wasn't stylish. I don't think anyone in their wildest dreams would think of him as sexy and <u>he certainly wasn't rich</u>. In fact, **he was struggling to make ends meet.**

Meaning…

Juicy story

(5) An idiom or collocation. You can treat it as a noun and ask: What is it?

(D) The question directs you to the next sentence where to find the specific details that tell you what a "juicy story" is.

(F) Note that this is a repetition of the idea expressed in "one of the juiciest pieces of gossip" in the first paragraph of the story. It is in a different form but if you didn't manage to work out the meaning the first time, you might succeed this time.

> So I was a little surprised during a dinner party one night when I first heard hints of **a juicy story** about Charlie and the Hollywood star. Nobody said it directly but they all implied that <u>he and Evelyn had had a love affair</u> during her visit a few weeks before.

Meaning…

Implied

(3) Verb. Ask: What action or state does it express and who or what does it refer to?

(E) Clearly, this refers to the narrator's friends. They are the ones who "implied" something. The clue is at the beginning of the sentence where, to clarify and emphasize the meaning, a contrast has been drawn between *saying* something directly and *implying* something and the linking word "but" is used to draw your attention to the contrast.

> <u>Nobody said it directly</u> but they all **implied** that he and Evelyn had had a love affair during her visit a few weeks before.

Meaning…

The Vocabulary Detective

Skeptical

(4) Adjective, so ask: Who does it describe and in what way?

(D) The answer to the first part of the question is that it describes "some of us" and explains their attitude towards the story. To find out exactly what that attitude was, and the meaning of "skeptical", keep reading and the second part of the sentence tells you how they explained their attitude themselves.

> Some of us were **skeptical** and <u>expressed doubt about the story</u>.

Meaning...

Unlikely couple

(5) Collocation. This is a combination of an adjective and a noun so ask: Who or what is it?

(B) There are two clues. One follows the collocation and is an expression with a similar meaning.

(E) The other clue is at the beginning of the sentence which refers you back to the first part of the story where Charlie and Evelyn are contrasted: she is described as famous, talented, sexy and very rich whereas he is the opposite of those things.

> <u>For the reasons mentioned above</u>, they were a most **unlikely couple** and the best that anyone could do to answer the question of what she saw in him was the old saying "<u>opposites attract</u>".

Meaning...

Skeptical

(F) This word is repeated, this time the narrator uses it to explain his attitude. There are two clues and, again, they are giving the specific details that explain what he means by "skeptical". If you didn't work it out last time, here is another chance. If you did work it out last time, you can check your understanding in this example.

> I'm a naturally **skeptical** person and I left the dinner party that night thinking that <u>something didn't add up</u>. I thought <u>it must have been a rumor</u>.

Meaning…
Something didn't add up
(5) A colloquial expression which provides a clue to the meaning of "skeptical" in the entry above. However, what it means may not be obvious because it has nothing to do with "adding up". Treat it as a verb and ask: What state does it express? And who or what does it refer to?

(D) The answer to the second question is what the narrator was thinking and this answer leads you to the specific details which form the clue to help you to unlock the meaning of the expression.

> I'm a naturally skeptical person and I left the dinner party that night thinking that **something didn't add up**. I thought it <u>must have been a rumor</u>.

Meaning…
Hit it off instantly
(5) Idiom. Treat this as a verb and ask: What state or action does it express and who does it refer to?

(B) The clue comes immediately afterwards in the form of an expression that is similar in meaning although slightly stronger and more specific. The idea is repeated for emphasis and clarity and the expression "you might even say" is used to advise you that a synonym is coming.

> It seemed they had **hit it off instantly**, you might even say it was <u>love at first sight</u>.

Meaning...

Speculation

(2) Noun. Ask: What was it? This should lead you to two clues.

(B) The first is the synonym "rumor". The linker "or" indicates that the meanings are very close and, in this context, almost interchangeable.

(E) To emphasize the point and make it even clearer, at the end of the sentence a contrast is drawn between "speculation" and "rumor", on one hand, and "truth" on the other.

> He claimed that nothing of what he said was **speculation** or <u>rumor</u>, it was <u>all true</u>.

Meaning...

Something that didn't quite add up

(F) This expression has already been used. If you could not work out the meaning before, here is another opportunity using a different type of clue. If you could work out the meaning before, here is an opportunity to check you understanding.

(B) This time the clue is a chunk of language with a similar meaning.

> It sounded believable the way Tony told it and it was a great piece of gossip to entertain your friends. But I still couldn´t help

thinking there was **something that didn't quite add up**. It seemed so unlikely.

Meaning...

Juicy

(F) This adjective is repeated so ask: What word does it qualify and in what way? The answer to the first question is obviously "gossip" which we have seen before but "juicy" here refers not to the details of the affair, as it did before, but to the fact that the affair between the Hollywood star and the humble reporter seemed so unlikely.

> But I still couldn't help thinking there was something that didn't quite add up. It just seemed so unlikely. Of course that was what made the gossip especially **juicy**.

Meaning...

Essence

(2) Noun. Ask: What was it? There are two clues.

(B) The collocation "basic details" is a synonym for "essence".

(D) The writer then spells out the specific details that make up the "essence" of the story.

> The **essence** always remained the same. The basic details were that they had met at a party, it was love at first sight, they had drunk Champagne and he had bought her flowers.

Meaning...

A lot of things that didn't add up

(F) The expression is used for the third time.

(E) This time the clue is a contrast in meaning, "the true story" contrasted to the one that "didn't add up".

> Still, there remained **a lot of things that didn't add up** so when I bumped into Charlie himself at a city bar one Friday night I couldn't wait to get the true story…

Meaning…

From the horse's mouth

(5) A colloquial expression. Ask: Who or what was the "horse's mouth" and what came from it?

(B) If you answer the second question first you will see that "the true story" was what came from the horse's mouth. And that is the clue that should help you to find the meaning of this strange expression. It follows that "the horse's mouth" is the person who is in the best position to know the truth. In other words, in this context, it is a synonym for Charlie.

> Still, there remained a lot of things that didn't add up so when I bumped into <u>Charlie himself</u> at a city bar one Friday night I couldn't wait to get the <u>true story</u> right **from the horse's mouth**.

Meaning…

Brush off

(5) This is an idiom that can be used as a noun or a verb. As it is a noun in this context, ask: What is it?

(D) The writer adds specific detail to make the meaning clear.

> "What's this I hear about you and Evelyn Somerset?" I said, expecting to get the **brush off**, <u>to be told to mind my own business</u>.

Meaning…

Juicy

(F) An adjective which has been used in one form or another three times before. Ask: What word does it modify in this context and in what way?

(D) This time it modifies the word "details" so to appreciate its meaning you need to look back in the story to identify the details that the writer regards as "juicy".

> "Do tell. What happened? All the **juicy** details please!"

Meaning…

Gauze

(2) Noun. So ask: What was it?

(B) The word "or" tells you that the meanings of "gauze" and "light cloth" are interchangeable, in other words they are synonyms.

> It contained a number of glass vials wrapped in **gauze** or <u>light cloth</u>.

Meaning…

Sniffed

(3) Verb. What action does it express and who or what does it refer to? The verb is used twice and refers first to Evelyn and then to the ordinary men and women.

(D) The clue is the detail that describes what Evelyn did before she sniffed.

> "With the champagne in her right hand, she reached into the box with her left hand, took out one of the vials, broke it open, <u>held it up to her nose</u> and **sniffed** it. 'Ahhhh,' she said and then offered the vial to the ordinary men and women surrounding her, each of whom also **sniffed** it. 'Great', 'Wow', 'Fantastic', 'Hey, man' was about all they could say.

Meaning…

A sniff

(F) One sentence later the same idea is repeated, only this time it is expressed as a noun. So ask: What is it?

(C) The question directs you to the clue which is a definition.

> "When it was my turn she told me to take **a sniff**, which I did, <u>inhaling the fumes up through my nose</u>.

Meaning…

Revive

(3) Verb. Ask: What action is expressed and who or what does it relate to?

(D) The answer to the second question is that it refers to the substance and to people having heart attacks. The clue to its meaning follows when the writer gives a specific detail.

> "I asked the man standing next to me what these thing were and he told me they were 'poppers', the party drug of the day which was really some kind of medicine used

to **revive** people having heart attacks. One sniff was supposed <u>to bring anyone back to life</u>."

Meaning…

Sniff

(F) Used for the third time. There is no clue here but if you look back to the previous mentions you should be able to work out what was going on.

> "One **sniff** was supposed to bring anyone back to life."

Meaning…

Snorting

(3) Verb. Ask: What action is being expressed and who or what does it refer to?

(B) The answer to the second question is that if refers to something that Evelyn was doing. To find out what you should look back in the story where you will see that "snorting" is a synonym for "sniffed" although with a very negative meaning in the context of taking illegal drugs.

> It had to be drunk but one bottle would be more than enough for Evelyn, especially with all those poppers she was **snorting**.

Meaning…

Humble

(4) Adjective. Ask: What word does it qualify and in what way?

(E) The answer is the "glass of beer" and the writer is drawing a contrast between the two drinks, champagne and beer. One is a luxurious drink and the other is not.

> But I must say, that <u>champagne was really good</u>. <u>Nectar of the gods, nectar of the gods</u>," he said raising a **humble** glass of beer to his lips.

Meaning...

The Lucky Number Fourteen

My most unforgettable Christmas Day was the one I spent with my father the year I left school. Dad was well known for his wisdom and commonsense and he needed both of those qualities on that day when we had two invitations to Christmas lunch. Whichever one he accepted, the other family was almost certain to be offended.

The first came from the Newtons, Jessie and Bob. They were quite old and although they were always very nice to me, Mrs. Newton was very **stern**. She was a bit like a strict school teacher and I wouldn't have dared to call her by her first name.

The other invitation came from the Jacksons, Mary and Mike. They were younger than the Newtons and more relaxed. If the choice had been mine, we would have gone to the Jacksons for Christmas lunch. What made their invitation especially attractive was their daughter Ellen who was about my age.

But, of course, the choice was not mine. And the decision was not as simple as it might seem. You see, Mrs. Newton and Mary were **rivals**. They both wanted to be the social leader in our community and they didn't like each other very much. In fact, **they couldn't stand each other**.

In the end father accepted Mrs. Newton's invitation because she had invited us first. I was disappointed and so was Mary but father, with his wise ways, managed to **smooth things over** with her and she invited us to come to her house for drinks before lunch.

Most of her lunch guests were already there when we arrived and, as it was Christmas Day, I was allowed to have a little beer. This helped me overcome my natural shyness and I chatted to Ellen for a little while.

I was really enjoying myself, and so was everyone else, when the phone rang. Ellen answered it and then held the receiver out to her mother and said "Mum, it's for you".

We could not help but hear Mary's voice as she answered the call but it wasn't so much what she said as the tone she adopted.

"Oh … oh … oh … oh," she said, obviously responding to some bad news in a tone that was a mixture of **distress** and **annoyance**. "Surely you can make the effort," she added angrily but clearly the answer was no. "Very well, then," she said curtly and slammed down the receiver.

She was obviously upset, I could see the tears welling up in her eyes. Everyone was looking at Mary, waiting for an explanation and it wasn't long in coming.

"That was Jim Bowden," she said with her voice shaking. "He says he's sick and won't be coming to lunch."

To me this seemed an overreaction. It was perfectly understandable that she would be disappointed, but there were plenty of other people there. It was hardly something to cry about. Another guest tried to ease the tension by making a joke out of it.

"That's great," he said with a laugh. "All the more for us!"

Mary was not amused. She stared **frostily** at the man who had made that comment.

"You don't understand," she said. "Without Jim we'll only have thirteen people at lunch. It will be terribly bad luck. What am I to do? What am I to do?"

Another guest tried to brush it off saying the idea that the number thirteen would bring bad luck was just a superstition, but Mary gave him a stare even frostier than the one she had directed at the joker. In fact, it was positively icy.

After that, a tense silence hung over the room. No one knew what to say. We could all see how upset and angry she was but some of us thought she was **overdoing it** and her superstition was a bit silly. Still, it was threatening to ruin the whole day until I had a bright idea which I thought was worthy of my father's famous wisdom and common sense.

"Why don't I stay here for Christmas lunch while dad goes on to the Newtons?" I said, my confidence well boosted by the two glasses of beer I had drunk. "That way you'll have fourteen people at the table after all."

As I spoke I noticed a look of horror on my father's face. He tried to stop me from going further but Mary didn't give him a chance. She grabbed me, hugged me and said I absolutely had to stay for lunch. There was no way that father was going to extract me from her **clutches**. Not only had I solved Mary's pressing problem and saved her Christmas lunch from being a gloomy affair, but there were plenty of benefits for me as well. I would avoid a long, boring lunch with the **stern** Mrs. Newton, instead I would spend afternoon with Ellen.

What made everything better was that I was suddenly treated as the guest of honor. Mary and Ellen pampered me and made sure that my wine glass was always full as we sat down to work our way through the Christmas **feast**. It was a real banquet with soup, turkey, ham, stuffing, gravy and cranberry sauce. And for dessert there would be a rich, heavy Christmas pudding with thick custard followed by cheese and port for anyone would could still eat.

But we had only just started the **feast** when the phone rang again.

"Hello," I heard Mary answer it and before long I recognized the same tone of anxiety tinged with **annoyance** that she had used when listening to Jim Bowden. "Oh … oh … oh …oh," she said. And finally: "Right, I'll get him for you."

She put the receiver down and came back into the dining room. Once again everyone had fallen silent. They were all looking at Mary but she was looking at me. "It's for you," she said **icily**.

I knew straight away that it was Mrs. Newton on the phone but I wasn't prepared for how angry and upset she was. Like Mary, she was superstitious and without me at her Christmas lunch she would have only 13 guests which would surely bring her bad luck. That was bad enough but what made it even worse was her belief that the misfortune should have been going the way of her great **rival**, Mary. And it was all my fault.

Luckily Mrs. Newton was not brief. She talked and talked. She ranted, she raved. She made threats. And, finally, she burst into tears. All of which gave me time to think up another bright idea.

By the time I got the chance to speak I had thought of a clever plan. "How about I have my main course here and then come around to your place for dessert? That way you'll have thirteen and a half people at your lunch and Mary will have the same."

It seemed like a great compromise to me. They would both be freed from the curse of the number thirteen. I couldn't help but congratulate myself once again on how well I was able to use the wisdom and common sense that I had inherited from my father.

"Okay," she said **sternly**. "But don't be long. I'll be expecting you in 45 minutes."

With that she hung up and I returned to the dining table. Almost everyone was looking at me, but not Ellen and her mother who were whispering to each other. I didn't catch what they were saying and I was very conscious that although Mrs. Newton had agree to the arrangement, Mary had not. But then again, like Mrs. Newton, she could hardly reject such a sensible, **diplomatic** compromise, so full of wisdom and common sense.

The lunch resumed with the main course but I didn't feel like the honored guest anymore. Now I was more like a captive who needed to be watched and guarded because he might escape at any moment. Not that I had any intention of **fleeing** before the main course. The food was fantastic. Mary and Ellen had prepared it and, I must say, they were great cooks.

They piled my plate high and when I had finished they offered me a second helping which I could not refuse. I looked at my watch after I had finished my **seconds** and said "I really must be going, time is ticking on". But before I could get up from the table, Mary took my plate away and, almost simultaneously, Ellen plonked in its place a great bowl of steaming Christmas pudding smothered with thick custard.

It was a well-planned piece of **teamwork** that happened so quickly I didn't have time to protest. But I realized what those two had been whispering about after my phone call with Mrs. Newton. They didn't care much for my carefully crafted **diplomatic** solution, they were definitely not going to have thirteen and a half diners at their table.

So I ate the Christmas pudding, and like everything else, it was delicious. When I had finished, I meekly and politely asked "Can I go now?"

"Of course you can, dear boy," said Mary. "It was lovely having you and do wish Jessie a happy Christmas from us." For the first time that day she really seemed happy.

So off I went to the Newtons' house. It was quite a long way but I didn't mind walking and, besides, I thought it might help to burn off some of the great Christmas lunch I had just eaten and make room for one more dessert.

Mrs. Newton answered the door when I arrived. She didn't raise her voice or shout or anything like that. She just spoke frostily, **icily**, sarcastically. "Come in young man, your lunch is ready." She led me along the hall, past the lounge room where the adults were having coffee and port. Not for the first time that day, I felt as though I was in the **spotlight** of general disapproval as I passed them and they stared at me through the doorway.

My destination was another great dining table, set for fourteen people. Thirteen of those places had been used and the table was littered with the remains of a great lunch: used glasses, napkins, some plates with leftovers on them, coffee cups, empty wine bottles.

But in the middle of the chaos, was a setting for the fourteenth diner. In other words, me. Mrs. Newton sat me down at my place and then disappeared into the kitchen. While I was waiting for her I couldn't help but notice there was a full set of **cutlery** in front of me. I had just expected a dessert spoon because that was the deal. I was only expecting to have dessert. But here there was a soup spoon, a knife and fork for the main course, a dessert spoon and fork and a small knife for the cheese and the bread.

I suspected that **something was up** and pretty soon my suspicions were confirmed. After a few minutes, Mrs. Newton emerged from the kitchen carrying a large bowl of soup. Yes, I was right. Like Mary, she had no intention of sticking to my carefully crafted compromise. I would have to eat, not just dessert, but a second full Christmas lunch within an hour of finishing the last one.

And so the food came. Mountains of it, the ham, the turkey, the roasted vegetables and all the trimmings: the stuffing, the gravy and the cranberry sauce. And finally the great, heavy, steamy Christmas pudding smothered in thick yellow custard and cream.

When it came to cooking, Mrs. Newton was certainly the equal of Mary and Ellen if not their **superior**. But under the circumstances I cannot say I enjoyed the meal. I thought I might be able to humor her by eating a small piece of each course and thus satisfy her need for fourteen diners. But she wouldn't allow that. I had to eat it all and, to make sure I didn't cheat in any way, she stood over me.

I could hear the **murmur** of conversation from the lounge room and although I couldn't make out exactly what they were saying, how I wished I could have joined my father and his friends but it was not to be. By the time I had finished, it was time to go home and I felt as though I was going to burst open.

The party broke up to a chorus of everyone wishing everyone else a happy Christmas. Mrs. Newton, like Mary before her, seemed especially happy, almost lighthearted. In the end she had had a happy Christmas.

As for me, I felt bloated and a little bit sick. My father never said a word about it. I guess he knew that I had learned an important lesson in life. He was the wise one, after all.

The Vocabulary Detective

Clues in the Context

Stern

(4) Adjective, so ask what word it qualifies and in what way?

(E) The answer to the first question is "Mrs. Newton" and the clue to the second question comes in the form of the comparison between her and a strict school teacher.

> Mrs. Newton was very **stern**. She was a bit like a strict school teacher and I wouldn't have dared to call her by her first name.

So what do you think it means?

Rivals

(2) Noun. Ask: What are they? There are two clues in the following sentence.

(D) The clues give details and specific examples of what "rivals" means in this context.

> Jessie and Mary were **rivals**. They both wanted to be the social leader in our community and they didn't like each other very much.

Meaning…

They couldn't stand each other

(5) This is a common colloquial expression which is effectively a verb. So ask: What action or state does it express and who does it relate to?

(B) The answer is, of course, that it relates to both Mrs. Newton and Mary and the clue to its meaning is in the previous sentence which contains a chunk of language very close in

50

meaning to "they couldn't stand each other". The idea has been repeated to emphasize that their dislike for each other was very strong.

> They both wanted to be the social leader in our community and <u>they didn't like each other very much</u>. In fact, **they couldn't stand each other**.

Meaning…

Smooth things over

(5) An idiom or multi-word verb. So ask: What action does it express and who does it refer to?

(D) It refers to the father and Mary. The clue comes in the specific detail later in the sentence when she was not upset after all.

> I was disappointed and so was Mary but father, with his wise ways, managed to **smooth things over** with her and <u>she invited us to come to her house for drinks before lunch</u>.

Meaning…

Distress / Annoyance

(2) Both are nouns. What are they? They are both close in meaning although not exactly the same. Both are used to convey as accurately as possible Mary's feelings.

(B) The first clue is the adverb "angrily" which describes the manner in which Mary spoke. Clearly she was angry and this would be a synonym for one of the two target words.

The Vocabulary Detective

(D) Other clues are in the way she ended the phone call and the description of her emotions. The question for the vocabulary detective to resolve is which of these details convey "distress" and which convey "annoyance".

> "Oh … oh … oh … oh," she said, obviously responding to some bad news in a tone that was a mixture of **distress** and **annoyance**. "Surely you can make the effort," she added <u>angrily</u> but clearly the answer was no. "Very well, then," she said curtly and slammed down the receiver.
>
> <u>She was obviously upset, I could see the tears welling up in her eyes</u>. Everyone was looking at Mary, waiting for an explanation and it wasn't long in coming.

Meaning of distress…
Meaning of annoyance…

Frostily

(4) Adverb so ask: What word does it qualify and how does it add meaning?

(B) The qualified word is "stared" so "frostily" tells you something about the way Mary stared at the man who made the joke. To get a clearer idea, keep reading and you will see a comparison with the stare she directed at the man who thought she was being superstitious. There you will find a synonym for "frostily" only with a stronger meaning.

> Mary was not amused. She stared **frostily** at the man who had made that comment.

"You don't understand," she said. "Without Jim we'll only have thirteen people at lunch. It will be terribly bad luck. What am I to do? What am I to do?"

Another guest tried to brush it off saying the idea that the number thirteen would bring bad luck was just a superstition, but Mary gave him a stare <u>even frostier</u> than the one she had directed at the joker. In fact, it was positively <u>icy</u>.

Meaning…

Overdoing it

(5) An idiom. Before asking any questions, study the expression to see if you can spot any clues.

(A) The verb "overdoing" is made up of two other words combined together: the prefix "over" means "too much" and the –ing form of the verb "do" which everyone should know.

(E) As "overdoing" is a verb ask: What action is being expressed here and who does it refer to? The question directs you to a contrast between the way Mary was behaving and the trivial nature of the problem. The contrast is signaled by the word "but".

We could all see how <u>upset and angry she was</u> but some of us thought she was **overdoing it** and <u>her superstition was a bit silly</u>.

Meaning…

Clutches

(2) Noun. What are they?

The Vocabulary Detective

(D) If you look at the previous sentence you will see the clue in the form of specific details and examples of Mary's behavior.

> <u>She grabbed me, hugged me and said I absolutely had to stay for lunch</u>. There was simply no way that father was going to extract me from her **clutches**.

Meaning...

Stern

(F) Second mention of this adjective, this time the clue to the meaning is the contrast drawn between Mrs. Newton and Ellen.

> I would avoid a long, boring lunch with the **stern** Mrs. Newton, instead I would spend the afternoon with <u>Ellen</u>.

Meaning...

Feast

(2) Noun. Ask: What is it? There are two clues.

(B) The first is in the next sentence and it is a synonym, "banquet". If you know what a banquet is, then you know what a "feast" is.

(D) But if you don't know either "feast" or "banquet" or you just want to check, read the rest of the following sentence which describes the meal in detail. These details should give you an idea of the meaning of "feast".

> Mary and Ellen pampered me and made sure that my wine glass was always full as we sat down to work our way through the **feast**.

The Lucky Number Fourteen

It was a real <u>banquet</u> with <u>soup, turkey, ham, stuffing, gravy and cranberry sauce. And for dessert there would be a rich, heavy Christmas pudding with thick custard followed by cheese and port for anyone would could still eat</u>.

But we had only just started the **feast** when the phone rang again.

Meaning…

Annoyance

(F) Repetition of this word in a different context. The clue is to look back at the first mention to reinforce your understanding of the word.

> "Hello," I heard Mary answer it and before long I recognized the same tone of **annoyance** that she had used when listening to Jim Bowden.

Meaning…

Icily

(4) Adverb, so ask: What word does it qualify and in what way? Is it positive or negative? The answer to the first question is that it qualifies the verb "said". It tells you something about the way in which Mary spoke. From the context you should be able to tell that it was negative.

(A) To get a more precise idea of the meaning, look at the word closely. It is an adverb that comes from the noun "ice" and this should help you get closer to the meaning.

The Vocabulary Detective

(F) Another clue is that you may remember the adjective "icy" was used previously as a stronger synonym for the adverb "frostily".

> They were all looking at Mary but she was looking at me. "It's for you," she said **icily**.

Meaning...

Rival

(F) Repeated mention, adding more detail about the competition between the two women on this particular day.

> I knew straight away that it was Mrs. Newton on the phone but I wasn't prepared for how angry and upset she was. Like Mary, she was superstitious and without me at her Christmas lunch she would have only 13 guests which would surely bring her bad luck. That was bad enough but <u>what made it even worse was her belief that the misfortune should have been going the way of</u> her great **rival**, <u>Mary</u>. And it was all my fault.

Meaning...

Sternly

(F) The third time this word appears, this time as an adverb qualifying "said". It tells you something about the way she said it. Unfortunately there is no clue nearby but to get the meaning look back to the two previous mentions when "stern" was used as an adjective.

> "Okay," she said **sternly**.

Meaning...

Diplomatic

(4) Adjective. What noun does it modify and in what way?

(B) The noun is "compromise" and it is modified by "diplomatic" and "sensible", two adjectives with similar meanings. So if you know what "sensible" means you will get close to "diplomatic" in this context. Two nouns used at the end of the sentence are also synonymous with "diplomatic" in this context.

> But then again, like Mrs. Newton, she could hardly reject such a sensible, **diplomatic** compromise, full of wisdom and common sense.

Meaning…

Fleeing

(3) Verb. What action is being expressed here and who does it refer to?

(B) It refers to the narrator of the story and in the previous sentence you will find a synonym.

> The lunch resumed with the main course but I didn't feel like the honored guest anymore. Now I was more like a captive who needed to be watched and guarded because he might escape at any moment. Not that I had any intention of **fleeing** before the main course.

Meaning…

Seconds

(2) Noun so ask: What are seconds? Context is especially important with this word because "seconds" is not a time reference as you might expect.

(B) The clue is that "seconds" is a repetition of "second helping" in the previous sentence.

> They piled my plate high and when I had finished they offered me a <u>second helping</u> which I could not refuse. I looked at my watch after I had finished my **seconds** and said "I really must be going, time is ticking on".

Meaning...

Teamwork
 (2) It is a noun, so ask: What is it?
(A) Before looking at the wider context, look at the word itself which is made from two words joined together, "team" and "work". You probably know both of these words and this should help you work out the meaning of the combined word.
(D) Now look at the wider context to see if you can find any other clues. Before and after the word "teamwork" you will find details and specific examples of what the word means in this context.

> But before I could get up from the table, <u>Mary took my plate away</u> and, <u>almost simultaneously, Ellen plonked in its place a great bowl of steaming Christmas pudding</u> smothered with thick custard.
>
> It was a <u>well-planned</u> piece of **teamwork** that happened so quickly I didn't have time to protest. <u>But I realized what those two had been whispering about</u> after my phone call with Mrs. Newton.

Meaning...

Diplomatic

(F) Second mention of this word in a slightly different context. It is an adjective so ask: What word does it qualify and in what way?

(D) The answer to the first question is "solution". The clue to the meaning follows when the detail of the solution is explained.

> They didn't care much for my carefully crafted **diplomatic** solution to a difficult problem, they were definitely not going <u>to have thirteen and a half diners at their table</u>.

Meaning…

Icily

(F) Repetition of the word. Used again as an adverb qualifying the way she spoke. As before, the word itself contains a clue to its meaning as it comes from the noun "ice". But this time there are other clues as well. Ask: What was special about the way she spoke?

(B) This directs you to two other adverbs that qualify "spoke". Both are synonyms of "icily".

> She didn't raise her voice or shout or anything like that. She just spoke <u>frostily</u>, **icily**, <u>sarcastically</u>.

Meaning…

Spotlight

(2) Noun. What does it refer to?

(D) The clue is the specific detail of what was happening. Everyone was looking at him.

The Vocabulary Detective

> I felt as though I was in the **spotlight** of general disapproval as I passed them and they stared at me through the doorway.

Meaning...

Cutlery

(2) Noun. Ask: What is it?

(D) The clue is a series of specific examples beginning with "dessert spoon". From these examples you should be able to work out what "cutlery" means.

> While I was waiting for her I couldn't help but notice there was a full set of **cutlery** in front of me. I had just expected a dessert spoon because I was only expecting to have dessert. But here there was a soup spoon, a knife and fork for the main course, a dessert spoon and fork and a small knife for the cheese and the bread.

Meaning...

Something was up

(5) Idiom which is the object of the verb "suspected". So ask: Exactly what did he suspect?

(D) In the same paragraph he gives specific details to help you understand the expression "something was up".

> I suspected that **something was up** and pretty soon my suspicions were confirmed. After a few minutes, Mrs. Newton emerged from the kitchen carrying a large bowl of soup. Yes, I was right. Like Mary, she had no intention of sticking to my carefully crafted

The Lucky Number Fourteen

<u>compromise. I would have to eat, not just dessert, but a second full Christmas lunch</u> within an hour of finishing the last one.

Meaning…

Superior

(2) This word can be an adjective but in this context it is used as a noun, so ask: What is it?

(E) The question should help you to notice that the writer is comparing and contrasting the cooking skills of the women. Comparison: Mrs. Newton was equal to Mary and Ellen. Contrast: Maybe she was superior. Is "a superior" the same as "an equal", or is it something more? The answer to that question should give you the meaning.

> When it came to cooking, Mrs. Newton was certainly <u>the equal</u> of Mary and Ellen if not their **superior**.

Meaning…

Murmur

(2) Noun. What is it? There are two clues here.

(D) From the specific details you can tell two things. First that it is a sound, it is something he heard. Second, the last few words of the sentence give you specific details that tell you something more about the sound. From that you get the meaning of "murmur".

> I could *hear* the **murmur** of conversation from the lounge room and <u>although I couldn't make out exactly what they were saying</u>…

Meaning

My Favourite Photo

If you came to our house you would be amazed by all the wildlife photos on the wall. From the front door right through to the lounge room, the walls are covered with my photography. It's like an art gallery but instead of paint, I use a camera.

There are pictures of monkeys as well as great sea creatures such as manatees, turtles, stingrays and sharks. There are iguanas and snakes. Creatures of all shapes and sizes, some **camouflaged** so you can hardly see them. Others in such bright colours that you can't miss them.

I always get lots of "oohs and ahs" when people come to our place for the first time. They love all of the pictures but there is one that stands out. It is of a jaguar and it hangs in pride of place over the mantelpiece in our living room.

People who see it for the first time always react positively. "Amazing picture," they say or "wow" or "that's fantastic". There's no doubt the jaguar picture is **a cut above the rest**. In fact it's even better than that, it's not just **a cut above the rest** it's head and shoulders above the rest, the cream of the crop, the icing on the cake or, better still, the crowning glory of my little exhibition.

The picture shows a jaguar in a tree. It is spotted, rather like a leopard, and in the dappled light of the forest its **camouflage** would make it hard to see but for one thing: it is looking straight at the camera as though it has just been startled. Its big, yellow eyes are wide with anxiety. I think "anxiety" is the best word although you could say something like **distress**, unease or disquiet.

Many people have told me the picture is so good that it ought to be on the cover of *National Geographic* magazine. Of course, I am flattered by all this. I **blush**, I turn red like an awkward teenager and never know what to say. It's a bit embarrassing really. I mean, I know the picture is very good but there is a story behind it which explains why I've never tried to publish it.

To understand how it **came about**, how the picture was taken, you have to go back to the beginning. Ever since I was a boy, I have been interested in photography. It's my hobby and my passion. I have travelled the world taking photos. You name a country and I've almost certainly been there and photographed it.

For a long time my specialty was **landscapes**. I loved the scenery of great mountains and forests, of rivers and deserts.

I carefully chose my best **landscape** photos, had them framed and hung them in our house. But the funny thing was that no one ever commented on them. Well, hardly anyone. I would get the occasional comment such as "nice picture" but it was said without great enthusiasm. I couldn't escape the impression that when they said something it was just to be polite but really they didn't think much of the pictures. Their comments were **damning with faint praise**.

Not even my wife commented on them and it was her silence that finally convinced me that the pictures were no good. She was kind-hearted and considerate and her philosophy was that if you had nothing good to say, then you should stay silent. So it was clear that she did not like the pictures either but if I wanted to find out why, I would have to ask her directly. So I did.

"What's wrong with my photos," I asked her one day. "Why don't people like them?"

"Oh, they're not so bad," she said, just like all the others, **damning with faint praise**.

"Come on, tell me straight. What's wrong with them? You don't like them. I can tell."

She sighed and she looked at me with an expression of sympathy.

"Well, technically they're very good," she said, "but …" and her voice trailed off as though she could not bear to hurt my feelings with what she was going to say next.

"But what?" I said sharply.

"They're **dull**," she said as sympathetically as she could.

"What do you mean '**dull**'?" I said. "'**Dull**' as in 'without colour' or '**dull**' as in 'boring'."

"The latter," she said. "Your photos are **dull** as in boring. They are uninteresting and unexciting. They're as dull as ditch water."

There was a long pause while I considered what she had said. I tried to think of some way of defending my pictures. Maybe they weren't as bad as she **made them out to be**. But, in the end, I was forced to admit she was right. I had to **concede**. There was no denying it, my photos were **dull**, **very dull**.

And, as usual, my wife had the answer. Her criticism was always **constructive**. That meant that if something was bad she didn't just say it was bad, she also provided ideas on how to fix it. In the case of my photography, her answer was clear. The big problem with my pictures was the subject matter. For some reason, views, **landscapes**, scenery or whatever you want to call them, are not very interesting subjects for photography. She

The Vocabulary Detective

suggested I should try taking wildlife pictures or pictures of people instead.

It was food for thought and I was still thinking how I might go about it when, a few days later, we had a visit from Ed Aitken, an old school friend of mine. I hadn't seen Ed in years and he hadn't changed much apart from going grey and getting a little thicker around the waist just like the rest of us.

His dress sense hadn't changed much either. He had been famous at school for wearing bright colours in strange combinations that didn't quite match. For instance, on the day he came to see us he was wearing a green shirt with an orange jacket which, to me, looked very strange.

Apart from his unusual sense of colour, Ed's big claim to fame at school was that he was born in Belize, a tiny country on the Caribbean coast of Central America just south of Mexico and to the east of Guatemala. The reason I hadn't seen him in years was that, instead of going from school to university like the rest of us, he had gone back to the country of his birth to work in his father's tourism business. He had been there ever since and now owned the business himself.

It was great to catch up with him and before leaving he invited us to come and stay with him on our next holiday.

Of course we accepted and of course I saw straight away the opportunity to try my hand at some wildlife photography and perhaps get a collection of pictures for our wall that was not **dull** and uninteresting but exactly the opposite, exciting, interesting, maybe even fascinating.

And so off we went, the very next summer. The weather was beautiful and Ed was a great host. Nothing was too much trouble for him and, thanks to his business connections, he was able to show us around his fascinating country. Ed took us to Altun Ha and Caracol, great centres of the old Mayan civilization which had **flourished** more than a thousand years ago. We were awestruck by the archaeological sites and the great temples.

But what interested me most was the wildlife. Ed took us out to Belize's Barrier Reef with all its little islands and its **fabulous variety** of exotic animals. I donned a mask and flippers and took my camera underwater and **shot** the pictures of manatees, turtles, stingrays and sharks that now grace the walls of our house.

I also **shot** lots of pictures of the bird life such as brightly coloured macaws and great eagles. And finally, there were the land animals. I managed to **shoot**, as in take pictures of, various monkeys and a big iguana. I especially loved the macaws. They were so bright and colourful with bright red heads and splashes of yellow and blue on their wings and bodies. But Ed didn't seem all that interested in them which I thought odd given his liking for bright, **clashing colours**.

But what I really wanted, above all, was a picture of a jaguar. I had never really thought about it before I went to Belize, but the more success I had with my wildlife pictures, the more I realized the ultimate achievement would be to get a picture of the famously elusive big cat in its natural **habitat**.

Inland from a town called Dangriga there is a 240 square kilometre wildlife park called the Cockscomb Wildlife Sanctuary where jaguars roam free in their natural environment. If I was going to photograph a jaguar, I would have to go there.

But everyone warned me that the chances of seeing a jaguar were so slight as to be hardly worth the trouble. They said the odds were about 17,000 to one. The jaguar's pale yellow fur with dark spots gives it a perfect **camouflage** in the sub-tropical jungle that is its natural home and it is very hard to see. But I had plenty of time and persuaded Ed to take me there.

We **tramped** – or as Ed would say hiked – through the jungle and into the mountains for hours. I had my camera at the ready the whole time because I knew that, in the unlikely event that we saw a jaguar, I would only get a very brief opportunity to take a picture.

And it was just as well that I was ready because Ed suddenly grabbed my sleeve and pointed to a tree up ahead of us. "There," he whispered.

"Where?" I whispered back. "I can't see anything."

"There, there. Up in the tree," whispered Ed.

But as hard as I looked into the dappled light of the forest, I still couldn't see anything.

"Here, give me the camera," said Ed. So I passed it too him and he lifted it up to his eye, pointed it at the tree and went "Click!"

The sharp sound of the shutter seemed to cut through the still silence of the jungle and then I saw it. The big cat turned its head in the direction of the sound and looked straight at us with its big, wide, startled eyes.

"Click!" went Ed with the camera again. And then he clicked for a third time and passed me the camera. But it was too late, the jaguar had gone.

"Sorry," said Ed. "I don't know anything about photography. I don't think they will come out very well. They're probably blurred."

We stood there for a moment trembling with fear because the jaguar could be very dangerous if cornered. It is the third biggest member of the cat family after lions and tigers and its jaws are immensely powerful. The thought of that made me nervous and, having seen one in the trees, I walked all the way back constantly looking up into the branches just in case.

My Favourite Photo

As soon as we got back to the place where we were staying, we checked the photos. I had to study the first image quite closely before I could make out the shape the jaguar stretched out on a branch looking sleepily away from us.

However, the second image was sharp and clear. There was no mistaking the jaguar thanks to the fact that it had turned its head in response to the click and was suddenly **alert** and looking straight at the camera. It was the animal's eyes that made the picture so **compelling**, you couldn't help but look at them and the photo not only preserves the image but also the emotional impact of the moment. Every time I look at it I recall the feeling of exhilaration and the tremor of fear I felt that day in the Belizean jungle.

The third image was nothing. In the split second it had taken Ed to press the button three times, the jaguar had gone.

I marvelled at how Ed had managed to spot it in the first place when I had difficulty trying to **make it out** from the first photo. I asked him how he could possibly have seen it. Did he have a sixth sense or something? Was it **intuition**?

But no, the answer was much simpler and I should have guessed. Ed was colour blind. That's why he often wore clothes with mismatching colours. That's why he didn't share our excitement at the brightly coloured macaws. They just looked **dull** to him. But when it came to stalking wildlife in the jungle, Ed had a huge advantage. He could see through nature's **camouflages**. The jaguar had been practically invisible to me, but to him it stood out as though there were a spotlight on it.

So that's the story of how the photo came to be taken and why I would never submit it for publication. I never actually claimed I took it, people just assumed that I had. But, of course, I never said I hadn't either. I allowed the impression to grow and I told myself that, in a way, it was my photo. I was the one who wanted to go looking for the jaguar while everyone else, including Ed, tried to discourage me. So I was the one who **persisted** and it was my camera and my settings. All Ed had to do was press the button which I would have done myself if only I had been able to see through the jaguar's disguise like he could.

Clues in the Context

Camouflaged

(4) Adjective so ask: what word does it modify and in what way? The answer to the first question is the creatures and there are two clues to the meaning.

(D) The first clue is the added detail that follows immediately and explains what is meant by "camouflaged".

(E) The second clue is a contrast between the camouflaged animals and the others.

> Creatures of all shapes and sizes, some **camouflaged** so <u>you can hardly see them</u>. Others in such bright colors that <u>you can't miss them</u>.

So what do you think it means?

A cut above the rest

(5) An idiomatic expression which is effectively an adjective describing the photo. So ask, what does it tell you about the picture?

(B) This question directs you to a series of colloquial expressions and collocations that are synonymous with "a cut above the rest". Not only that, but there are also clues to the relative strength of each expression. The linking phrase "even better than that" tells you that the next three expressions are stronger than "a cut above the rest" and the linking phrase "better still" tells you that "crowning glory" is the strongest of all.

> There's no doubt the jaguar picture is **a cut above the rest**. In fact it's even better than that, it's not just **a cut above the rest** it's

> head and shoulders above the rest, the cream of the crop, the icing on the cake or, better still, the crowning glory of my little exhibition.

Meaning…

Camouflage

(F) The word is repeated but this time it is used as a noun. So ask: What is it?

(D) Again, the clue is a detail that tells you the effect of the camouflage and therefore should help you to work out the meaning.

> It is spotted, rather like a leopard, and in the dappled light of the forest its **camouflage** would make it hard to see but for one thing: it is looking straight at the camera as though it has just been startled.

Meaning…

Distress

(2) Noun. What is it?

(B) The clues come in the form of a number of synonyms giving a range of meaning but the preferred one in this context is "anxiety".

(F) Note that this word also appears in *The Lucky Number Fourteen* in a different context with a slightly different meaning illustrated by specific details.

> I think "anxiety" is the best word although you could say something like **distress**, unease or disquiet.

Meaning…

Blush

(3) A verb so ask: what action is being expressed and who does it refer to?

(D) In the same sentence and the next one, extra details are added that explain what is meant by "blush" in this context.

> I **blush**, I <u>turn red</u> like an awkward teenager and never know what to say. It's a bit <u>embarrassing</u> really.

Meaning…

Came about

(5) Idiom, a multi-word verb so ask: What action does it express and who or what does it refer to?

(B) The text gives you a clue when the meaning is repeated using what is, in the context, a synonym.

> To understand how it **came about**, <u>how the picture was taken</u>, you have to go back to the beginning.

Meaning…

Landscapes

(2) A noun used in the plural form so ask: What are they?

(D) The clues are specific details and examples of the things that the narrator liked photographing.

> For a long time my specialty was **landscapes**. I loved the <u>scenery</u> of <u>great mountains</u> and <u>forests</u>, of <u>rivers</u> and <u>deserts</u>.

Meaning…

Landscape

(F) The word is repeated but this time used as an adjective.

> I carefully chose my best **landscape** photos, had them framed and hung them in our house.

Meaning...

Damning with faint praise

(5) An idiomatic expression which is, effectively, a verb. So ask: what action is being expressed and who is doing it? The expression is used twice and the first time it refers to the guests who came to the narrator's house and the second time to his wife.

(B) The first clue to the meaning is a synonym: "they didn't think much of the pictures".

(D) There are a number of other clues as well in the form of details and specific examples of what the guests and the wife thought of the pictures.

> I would get the occasional comment such as "nice picture" but it was said without great enthusiasm. I couldn't escape the impression when they said something it was just to be polite but really they didn't think much of the pictures. Their comments were **damning with faint praise**.
>
> Not even my wife commented on them and it was her silence that finally convinced me that the pictures were no good. She was kind-hearted and considerate and her philosophy was that if you had nothing good to say, then you should stay silent. So it was

clear that she did not like the pictures either but if I wanted to find out why, I would have to ask her directly. So I did.

"What's wrong with my photos," I asked her one day. "Why don't people like them?"

"Oh, they're not so bad," she said, just like all the others, **damning with faint praise**.

Meaning…

Dull

(4) Adjective. What word does it qualify and in what way? There are three clues.

(C) The first two clues are in the dialogue where the husband asks her directly for the meaning and gives two possible definitions.

(D) The third clue comes in the next paragraph where she chooses the second of the husband's definitions and goes on to give details that explain specifically what she means. Included is the colloquial expression "dull as ditch water" used here for emphasis.

"They're **dull**," she said as sympathetically as she could.

"What do you mean '**dull**'?" I said. "'**Dull**' as in 'without color' or '**dull**' as in 'boring'."

"The latter," she said. "Your photos are **dull** as in boring. They are uninteresting and unexciting. They're as dull as ditch water."

Meaning…

Made them out to be

(5) Multi word verb. Who is the subject of this verb? It is she, the wife. So ask: What did she do?

(B) The clue is at the beginning of the paragraph. "She made them out to be" is a synonym for "she had said".

> There was a long pause while I considered what <u>she had said</u>. I tried to think of some way of defending my pictures. Maybe they weren't as bad as she **made them out to be**.

Meaning…

Concede

(3) Verb. What action is expressed and who or what does it refer to?

(B) It was something that the narrator did or said and the meaning is expressed twice, once using "concede" and once using a synonym.

> But, in the end, I was forced to <u>admit</u> she was right. I had to **concede**. There was no denying it, my photos were dull, very dull.

Meaning…

Dull

(F) Repetition of the word.

> There was no denying it, my photos were **dull**, **very dull**.

Meaning…

Constructive

(3) Adjective. What does it qualify and in what way? The answer to the first part of the question is that it qualifies the meaning of "criticism". There are two clues to help you answer the second part of the question.

(C) The first clue is a clear definition of the word, signalled by the words "that meant".

(D) The second includes details and specific examples to explain how her criticism was constructive.

> Her criticism was always **constructive**. That meant that <u>if something was bad she didn't just say it was bad, she also provided ideas on how to fix it</u>. In the case of my photography, her answer was clear. The big problem with my pictures was the subject matter. For some reason, views, landscapes, scenery or whatever you want to call them, are not very interesting subjects for photography. <u>She suggested I should try taking wildlife pictures or pictures of people instead</u>.

Meaning...

Landscapes

(F) Repetition with synonyms.

> For some reason, <u>views</u>, **landscapes**, <u>scenery</u> or whatever you want to call them, are not very interesting subjects for photography.

Meaning...

The Vocabulary Detective

Dull

(F) Repetition. This time with two clues. The first is a synonym and the second a series of contrasting adjectives signalled by the linking phrase "exactly the opposite".

> Of course we accepted and of course I saw straight away the opportunity to try my hand at some wildlife photography and perhaps get a collection of pictures for our wall that was not **dull** and uninteresting but exactly the opposite, exciting, interesting, maybe even fascinating.

Meaning...

Flourished

(3) Verb. Ask: What action or state does it express and who or what does it refer to? The answer to the second part of the question is that this refers to the Mayan civilization in Central America. So how did it flourish?

(D) The clue is an example of what is meant by "flourished".

> Ed took us to Altun Ha and Caracol which had been great centres of the old Mayan civilization which had **flourished** more than a thousand years ago. We were awestruck by the archaeological sites and the great temples.

Meaning...

Fabulous variety

(5) Collocation made from an adjective and a noun. Ask about the noun first: What is it? Then ask about the adjective: In what way does it qualify the meaning of the noun?

(D) The clues to help you answer these questions are in the form of specific examples of what he meant.

> Ed took us out to Belize's Barrier Reef with all its little islands and its **fabulous variety** of exotic animals. I donned a mask and flippers and took my camera underwater and shot the pictures of manatees, turtles, stingrays and sharks that now grace the walls of our house.
>
> I also shot lots of pictures of the bird life such as brightly coloured macaws and great eagles. And finally, there were the land animals. I managed to shoot, as in take pictures of, various monkeys and a big iguana. I especially loved the macaws. They were so bright and colourful with bright red heads and splashes of yellow and blue on their wings and bodies.

Meaning…

Shoot / shot

(3) Verb. So ask: What action is being expressed here and who or what does it refer to?

(C) This is a very good example of a word taking its meaning from the context. The primary meaning of the verb "shoot" is to fire a gun but that is not what is meant here and to make it absolutely clear that he was not shooting the animals with a rifle, the narrator gives a definition of what he means.

The Vocabulary Detective

(D) He also gives specific examples and details to make his meaning clear.

> I donned a mask and flippers and took my <u>camera</u> underwater and **shot** the <u>pictures</u> of manatees, turtles, stingrays and sharks that now grace the walls of our house.
>
> I also **shot** lots of <u>pictures</u> of the bird life such as brightly coloured macaws and great eagles. And finally, there were the land animals. I managed to **shoot**, <u>as in take pictures of</u>, various monkeys and a big iguana.

Meaning…

Clashing colours

(5) Collocation. Again, an adjective and a noun. You should know "colours" so ask: What was special or different about these colours?

(D) To get the answer you have to go back in the story to the description of Ed when he was first mentioned. The description contains examples

> He had been famous at school for wearing <u>bright colours in strange combinations that didn't quite match</u>. For instance, on the day he came to see us he was wearing <u>a green shirt with an orange jacket</u> which, to me, looked very strange.
>
> ….
>
> But Ed didn't seem all that interested in them which I thought odd given his liking for bright, **clashing colours**.

Meaning…

Habitat

(2) Noun. What is it?

(B) The idea is repeated twice in the next two paragraphs using synonyms.

>...the ultimate achievement would be to get a picture of the famously elusive big cat in its natural **habitat**.
>
>Inland from a town called Dangriga there is a 240 square kilometre wildlife park called the Cockscomb Wildlife Sanctuary where jaguars roam free in their natural environment. If I was going to photograph a jaguar, I would have to go there.
>
>But everyone warned me that the chances of seeing a jaguar were so slight as to be hardly worth the trouble. They said the odds were about 17,000 to one. The jaguar's pale yellow fur with dark spots gives it a perfect camouflage in the sub-tropical jungle that is its natural home and it is very hard to see.

Meaning…
Camouflage

(F) Repetition, again as a noun and again with a specific detail to check the meaning.

>The jaguar's pale yellow fur with dark spots gives it a perfect **camouflage** in the sub-tropical jungle that is its natural home and it is very hard to see.

Meaning…

The Vocabulary Detective

Tramped

(3) Verb so ask: What action does it express and who was doing it? The answer to the second part of the question is that it was the narrator and Ed who performed this action and there are two clues to the meaning.

(B) The first clue is the synonym "hiked".

(D) The second clue is made up of the specific details describing where they went.

> We **tramped** – or as Ed would say <u>hiked</u> – <u>through the jungle</u> and <u>into the mountains</u> for hours.

Meaning…

Alert

(4) Adjective. Ask: What word does it qualify and in what way?

(D) "Alert" is used to describe the jaguar. There are two clues to help you work out the meaning. Both are specific details describing the jaguar's behaviour. The first is several paragraphs before "alert" appears in the text when the jaguar's reaction to the sound of the camera is first described.

> The sharp sound of the shutter seemed to cut through the still silence of the jungle and then I saw it: The big cat turned its head in the direction of the sound and <u>looked straight at us with its big, wide, startled eyes</u>.

The second clue comes immediately after the word "alert":
> There was no mistaking the jaguar thanks to the fact that it had turned its head in response to the click and was suddenly **alert** and <u>looking straight at the camera</u>.

Meaning…

Compelling

(4) Adjective describing the picture. Ask: What special quality did the picture have?

(C) In very next phrase there is a clue which spells out exactly what he meant by "compelling".

> It was the animal's eyes that made the picture so **compelling**, <u>you couldn't help but look at them</u>.

Meaning…

Make it out

(5) Multi word verb, colloquial expression which is very similar to "made it out to be" (above) but means something different. The best way to tell the difference is from the context. So ask: What action or state does it express? And who or what does it refer to?

(B) The expression refers to the narrator and there are two clues, both of them synonyms for what Ed was able to do and what the narrator could not do.

> I marvelled at how Ed had managed to <u>spot it</u> in the first place when I had difficulty trying to **make it out** from the first photo. I asked him how he could possibly have <u>seen it</u>.

Meaning…

Intuition

(2) Noun. What is it?

(B) It is a repeat of the idea of "a sixth sense".

> Did he have <u>a sixth sense</u> or something? Was it **intuition**?

Meaning…

The Vocabulary Detective

Dull

(F) Repetition but this time used with a slightly different meaning. In all the previous mentions the sense was "uninteresting" but this time it is used in the sense of "lacking colour". The clue is in the contrast between the way narrator and his wife saw the colourful macaws and the way Ed saw them.

> But no, that answer was much simpler and I should have guessed. Ed was color blind. That's why he often wore clothes with mismatching colors. That's why <u>he didn't share our excitement at the brightly colored macaws</u>. They just looked **dull** to him.

Meaning...

Camouflages

(F) Repetition. This time it is used as a plural noun and the clues to the meaning lie in the details given before and after the word is used.

> But when it came to stalking wildlife in the jungle, Ed had a huge advantage. <u>He could see through</u> nature's **camouflages**. The jaguar had been <u>practically invisible to me, but to him it stood out as though there were a spotlight on it</u>.

Meaning...

Persisted

(3) Verb. Ask: What action or state does it express? Who does it refer to?

84

(D) The clue is in the previous sentence when the narrator describes how he was the person who insisted on looking for the jaguar when everyone else tried to discourage him. "Persisted" is a repetition of this idea.

> I was the one who wanted to go looking for the jaguar while everyone else, including Ed, tried to discourage me because it was a waste of time. So I was the one who **persisted** and it was my camera and my settings.

Meaning...

Devil in the Detail

They say that experience is better than book learning. You can understand something by studying it in a book but you don't really *know* it until you experience it. Let me give you an example. When I was a young reporter at a big newspaper many years ago they always told us to check our facts.

"Always remember," said the editor, "the devil is in the detail. It's the small things that sometimes trip you up."

And of course I understood that this was very, very important but I didn't fully understand, I didn't really *know* how important it was until I had the experience of getting something wrong. It was only a small mistake but it had big consequences.

My experience began on a quiet Sunday in the office. I was by far the most junior reporter on duty that day. I had only just been promoted from the job of copy boy. As a copy boy I used to make the tea and **run errands**. A typical day involved getting takeaway lunches for all the senior staff as well as carrying messages around the office. But now I was ready to actually write reports for the newspaper and I was very eager to have my first story published.

That Sunday I got my opportunity. The chief reporter wanted someone to do a story about a major exhibition that was due to open at the city art gallery. None of the senior reporters wanted to do it. They were not interested in art, they preferred to cover crime stories or football.

But I was keen, not just because I wanted to get my first story into the paper but because the artist was Amedeo Modigliani. I didn't know much about art in those days but I had just read a biography of Modigliani and was totally fascinated, in fact **captivated,** by his life story and his paintings so I didn't need to do much research, I already knew a lot about him. You could say **I had all the facts at my fingertips.**

Modigliani was born in Italy in 1884 and went to Paris as a young man where he became part of the avant-garde movement in art. He lived an exciting life and painted lots of pictures, mainly portraits and nudes but it was only after his death from tuberculosis in 1920 that his paintings became famous.

Those were the basic facts but I interviewed the director of the art gallery, Dr. Seddon McRobie to get an expert view and to ask him why people did not like Modigliani´s paintings at first.

"What you have to understand is that he was completely original," said McRobie, a **nattily dressed** man who always wore a bow tie and spoke very quickly. "No one had ever seen anything like this before and it took some getting used to.

"If you look at his paintings you will see that he **distorted** the human form by stretching the features and characteristics of his subjects: their faces and necks and even their bodies. His **elongated** style was enormously **influential** and you see many other artists doing similar things now, but in the early twentieth century it was completely new and no one really understood it.

"We are very lucky to have a **comprehensive** exhibition of his work which covers every aspect of his enormous talent from the time he arrived in Paris until his untimely death at just 35 years of age. No one should miss this opportunity to see for themselves some of the best work of one of the greatest artists of the twentieth century. Indeed, one of the greatest artists of all time."

And so I wrote my story. Six-hundred words on the genius and his work and **quoting** Dr McRobie. "An exhibition not to be missed," he said. Included with my report were four or five pictures from the exhibition of Modigliani's long-necked people and of course, for the benefit of the art lovers among our readers, I included the essential fact that the exhibition would be open to the public from 9am on Monday morning.

That morning I was up early to get the paper and I was not disappointed by the results. There was my story spread across two pages with big pictures and my name on it! I had been the most junior reporter in the office on Sunday, and yet on Monday I had far more in the paper than any of the senior reporters. And this was just my first attempt!

I went to work that day **buzzing** with excitement and expecting to get congratulations from my boss so I was not surprised when I was called into the editor's office.

As I expected, he congratulated me on the report in the paper.

"Nice job," he said. "But there's just one problem." My heart sank. A problem? How could that be? I had checked my facts over and over again.

"Oh," I responded, trying not to seem too nervous.

"Yes, you say the exhibition opens this morning," he said and he looked **stern**, like a strict teacher in school.

"Yes, that's right," I replied, "nine o'clock this morning."

"No, that's not right," said the editor. "Dr. Seddon McRobie himself has been on the phone to me and he tells me it doesn't open this morning, the opening is *next* Monday. And he's very, very angry. In fact, he was shouting down the phone."

The Vocabulary Detective

I didn't know what to say. The editor just stood and **glared** at me in silence. Although I felt very uncomfortable with my boss looking at me angrily like that, to be honest I couldn't really see what all the **fuss** was about at first. Sure, it was a mistake but it was only a small mistake, one small detail in a few hundred words.

"Maybe we could just run a correction," I said in a nervous voice. "It's only a detail."

The editor sighed.

"Yes, we'll put a correction and an apology in the paper tomorrow," he said.

"Why do we have to apologize," I said. "It's just a detail."

He sighed again. More deeply this time.

"You should know that the devil is in the detail," he said. "I'm sure I told you this last week before you were promoted from copy boy to reporter. It's the small details that can get you into trouble if you get them wrong. And there are consequences."

That sounded **ominous**, almost threatening.

"Consequences?" I said nervously.

"For a start, there were 300 people queued outside the gallery at nine o'clock this morning to see an exhibition of Modigliani paintings that doesn't open until next week."

Now I began to understand. Experience was teaching me something that had not seemed obvious before. Small details could be very dangerous if you got them wrong. It wasn't just Dr. McRobie and the editor who were angry, so were hundreds, possibly thousands, of people who had made plans to see the exhibition and now had to change their arrangements.

The complaints were pouring in to the editor's office. Much of what they said was unprintable but the general sense of it was that I was stupid and incompetent and if I couldn't get a simple fact right, then everything else I had written must have been full of mistakes as well.

And there was worse to come for me. The editor told me that I needed to take some time to reflect on what I had done and so I was demoted to my old position of copy boy. I had to go back to making the tea and running errands.

And so I learned my lesson. Not from anything I had been told, but from experience. The devil really was in the detail and he made me pay a heavy price for my little mistake.

The Vocabulary Detective

Clues in the Context

Run errands

(5) This is an idiom and the key word is the verb "run" so ask: What action does it express and who or what does it refer to?

(D) Those questions are answered by the clues in the next sentence, specific details to help you work out the meaning.

> As a copy boy I used to make the tea and **run errands**. A typical day involved getting takeaway lunches for all the senior staff as well as carrying messages around the office.

So what do you think it means?

Captivated

(3) Passive verb so ask: Who or what does it refer to and in what way?

(B) The answer to the first question is that it refers to the way the life story of the artist affected the narrator of the story. The clue is the phrase "totally fascinated" which is a synonym for "captivated". For emphasis and clarity the same idea is repeated using a different, but slightly stronger, word.

> I had just read a biography of Modigliani and was totally fascinated, in fact **captivated,** by his life story.

Meaning…

I had all the facts at my fingertips

(5) An idiom which begins with the verb "had" so ask: What state does it express? And what does it refer to? There are two clues.

(B) The first clue is a synonymous expression. The sentence "I already knew a lot about him" is synonymous with "I had all the facts at my fingertips" and the writer gives a big hint of the similarity when he says "you could say".

(D) The second clue gives the specific details of exactly what he had, the facts that he is referring to.

> <u>I already knew a lot about him</u>. You could say **I had all the facts at my fingertips.**
>
> <u>Modigliani was born in Italy in 1884 and went to Paris as a young man where he became part of the avant-garde movement in art. He lived an exciting life and painted lots of pictures, mainly portraits and nudes</u>…

Meaning…

Nattily dressed

(5) An idiom which acts as an adjective. So ask: What word does it qualify?

(D) The answer is that it describes McRobie and to find out how, you should look at the specific details that follow: he always wore a bow tie. This gives you a clue to the meaning of "nattily dressed".

> …said McRobie, a **nattily dressed** man who <u>always wore a bow tie</u>…

Meaning…

The Vocabulary Detective

Distorted

(3) A verb so ask: What action or state does it express? And who does it refer to? The answers to these questions is that he refers to Modigliani and the way he painted people.

(B) The clue is the verb "stretching" which is a synonym for "distorted" or "distorting".

> "If you look at his paintings you will see that he **distorted** the human form by stretching the features and characteristics of his subjects: their faces and necks and even their bodies.

Meaning...

Elongated

(4) An adjective so ask: What word does it qualify and how does it modify the meaning? Obviously it qualifies the noun "style" and there are two clues.

(B) The clues are the synonyms that you have already seen in the previous sentence: "distorted" and "stretching". "Elongated" expresses the same meaning, though in the form of an adjective. It is used to avoid repetition.

> "If you look at his paintings and his sculptures you will see that he distorted the human form by stretching the features and characteristics of his subjects: their faces and necks and even their bodies. His **elongated** style ...

Meaning...

Influential

(4) An adjective so ask again: What word does it qualify and in what way?

(A) Before looking at the context you might notice that the adjective "influential" is related to the noun "influence" and the verb "to influence".

(D) Like "elongated" it qualifies the noun "style" but in a different way. This time the question leads you to specific details that follow "influential".

> His elongated style was enormously **influential** and you see many other artists doing similar things now, but in the early twentieth century it was completely new and so people found it hard to get used to.

Meaning…

Comprehensive

(4) An adjective. What word does it qualify? And how does it modify the meaning?

(D) The questions direct you first to the noun "exhibition" and then to the end of the sentence where you find the clue in the form of specific details.

> "We are very lucky to have a **comprehensive** exhibition of his work which covers every aspect of his enormous talent from the time he arrived in Paris until his untimely death at just 35 years of age."

Meaning…

Quoting

(3) A verb so ask: What action does it express? And who or what does it refer to?

(A) Before looking at the context you might note that this present participle of the verb "to quote" is related to the noun "quotation".

(D) The answer to those questions tells you that it is something the journalist wrote and that leads you to the clue which tells you specifically what it was.

> And so I wrote my story. Six-hundred words on the genius and his work and **quoting** Dr. McRobie. "An exhibition not to be missed," he said.

Meaning…

Buzzing

(3) Verb. So ask: Who what action or state does this express? And who or what does it refer to?

(D) The answers to these questions tell you that the verb refers to the narrator, the young journalist, and it expresses his state of mind or mood at the time. These answers lead you to the clues which are specific details.

> I went to work that day **buzzing** with excitement and expecting to get congratulations from my boss.

Meaning…

Stern

(4) Adjective so ask: What word does it modify and in what way?

(E) The adjective is used to describe the editor and the clue to its meaning is in the comparison with "a strict teacher".

(F) You should note that the same word, with the same comparison to a strict teacher, is used to describe Mrs. Newton in *The Lucky Number Fourteen*.

> "Yes, you say the exhibition opens this morning," he said and he looked **stern**, like a strict teacher in school.

Meaning…

Glared

(3) Verb. What state or action is expressed? Who or what does it refer to?

(C) It is something that the editor is doing. The clue comes in the next sentence which is a definition.

> The editor just stood and **glared** at me in silence. Although I felt very uncomfortable with my boss looking at me angrily like that…

Meaning…

Fuss

(2) Noun. So ask: What was it?

(D) It is clearly a reference to what is happening in the story so look back a few paragraphs and you will see the specific details that make this a "fuss": the reporter has made a mistake, the director of the Art Gallery is angry and so is the editor.

"Dr. Seddon McRobie himself has been on the phone to me and he tells me it doesn't open this morning, the opening is *next* Monday. And he's very, very angry. In fact, he was shouting down the phone."

I didn't know what to say. The editor just stood and glared at me in silence. Although I felt very uncomfortable with my boss looking at me angrily like that, to be honest I couldn't really see what all the **fuss** was about at first.

Meaning…

Ominous

(4) Adjective. What words does it qualify and in what way? Was it positive or negative? Once you have answered these questions, you should find two clues.

(B) One of the clues is the phrase "almost threatening" which synonymous with "ominous". The idea is repeated for emphasis using different words.

(D) The other clue is the specific detail in what the editor said. Clearly it was negative.

"I'm sure I told you this last week before you were promoted from copy boy to reporter. It's the small details that can get you into trouble if you get them wrong. And there are consequences."

That sounded **ominous**, almost threatening.

Meaning…

The Buffalo's Dilemma

It had been a fantastic barbecue. As always the professor was in charge of the meat and he had cooked a rolled joint of lamb on the spit until it was done to a turn, succulent and dripping with flavour.

To his friends, Professor Robin Hapgood was "the man who knows everything". Even though he was a famous professor at a famous university, this was **not meant as a compliment**. Many thought he was just a know-it-all, the kind of man who loved the sound of his own voice which he used to trumpet his own opinions and drown out the ideas and views of other people.

What made it worse, and even embarrassing at times for his wife and friends, was that he did not always know what he was talking about. People suspected that he sometimes just made things up so that he would sound cleverer than everyone else.

In regard to the question of whether the professor was just a loud-mouthed show-off, there was never any general agreement. But despite that, everyone agreed that, when it came to cooking meat on a barbecue, no one knew more or had greater skill than the learned professor.

His wife Maggie, also a university professor though a less pompous one, was the perfect partner for him in hosting a barbecue. His great talent was meat, hers was salads and, as always, she had prepared a great spread of green-leaf and tomato salads dressed with olive oil and wine vinegar and garnished with oregano from her herb garden. They were as good to look at as they were to eat and formed the perfect accompaniment to the **tender lamb**.

Their guests at the dinner were their old friends Tony and Liz. He brought the wine and she brought a fresh fruit salad for dessert.

"That was so sweet," said Maggie, **complimenting** Liz for her fruit salad.

"Yes, the perfect ending for a perfect meal," said the professor, "and I would say the only thing sweeter than that dessert is the relief we feel at being out of lockdown."

The professor was breaking a taboo when he said that. They had all agreed that the subject of the pandemic and the lockdown was off-limits for their barbecue. The idea was that it should be a happy occasion, a relief that finally the lockdown was over and life could start moving back to some sort of **normality** and eventually everything would be like it had been before.

But that was the professor all over. He couldn't help himself. He would always relate ordinary, everyday things and events to the great questions of the day whether in politics, science or the arts. He turned everything into an opportunity to show how clever he was.

And so the conversation turned to how hard it had been for everyone. They had been **confined** to their homes for six weeks in an attempt to stop the spread of the deadly pandemic. They were only allowed out to do the shopping or go to medical appointments. It was almost like being in prison, they agreed. The worst thing was the **loneliness**, being separated from family and friends.

"Indeed," said the professor. "It was Aristotle who declared that man was a social animal. Human contact is essential to our wellbeing."

"We're not just social animals, we're trading animals as well," said Tony. He and Liz ran their own stationery business on the high street and they were feeling the economic consequences acutely. "This lockdown has done enormous damage to our business and the economy generally. We may never recover, we might not survive. I think this lockdown was a terrible mistake and we'll be feeling the consequences for years to come."

"But what about lives?" said Maggie. "Surely we should put people's lives first. Without the lockdown thousands would have died."

"All I'm saying is there has to be a better way," said Tony. "The economy matters too, people's livelihoods matter too." For Tony and Liz it was, of course, personal. The business that they had worked all their lives to build was under threat. "There's a price to be paid for this and it's people like us who are going to pay it," said Tony, raising his voice.

"You and all the thousands of people who are losing their jobs. It's not just about you, Tony." Maggie, too, raised her voice. The argument was getting louder so the professor stepped in to settle the matter.

"Of course, there are good arguments on both sides of this question," he said sounding like a high-court judge delivering his judgment on a case of great importance. "On the one hand we must try to stop the spread of the pandemic and save lives. On the other there is the question of livelihoods. If we shut down the economy we destroy businesses and throw lots of people out of work, causing lots of **hardship**, many people won't be able to pay their rent or even put food on the table. Either way there

The Vocabulary Detective

is a cost, there is a price to pay in money and lives. It is a true **dilemma**, there is no easy answer."

"A what?" said Liz who had had a little bit too much to drink and hadn't really been paying much attention to the professor's lecture.

"A **dilemma**, is a special kind of problem. It's the kind of problem you have when there are two courses of action available to you and *both* of them are bad." said the professor who was only too happy to explain. "In this case the **dilemma** is clear, we have a choice between saving lives and saving the economy. We can't do both. As they saying goes, we are caught on the horns of a **dilemma**."

What had started as a conversation among old friends had suddenly turned into an argument and was now threatening to blow up into a full-scale row.

"Isn't this all a bit too depressing?" said Liz grumpily.

"Yes, Liz," said Maggie trying to calm everyone down. "But we have to be realistic. Life is tough. Life is full of predicaments, problems and yes, even dilemmas. Isn't life all about how we navigate around or through the many problems we face? Let's be realistic."

"Oh, I suppose so, Maggie," said Liz with a sigh. "But do we have to be quite so realistic now. Come on, we've just come out of a six-week lockdown, we haven't seen each other for ages. Can't we just **lighten up** a little? Can't we talk about something less depressing? Something light, something amusing, something entertaining. Something that's not so damn gloomy."

"Like what?" said Maggie.

"What did you have in mind?" said the professor at almost the same time.

"Oh, I don't know ... seen any good animal videos on You Tube lately?"

Everyone laughed except the professor who had nothing but **contempt** for You Tube animal videos. To him, they were trivial and a complete waste of time.

"Well, as a matter of fact I have," said Maggie, ignoring her aloof husband. "I saw this amazing video of a family in a wildlife park somewhere in Africa. They got out of the car to have a picnic when they were attacked by cheetahs. They were lucky to get out alive!"

"Oh, I can top that," said Tony. "I watched this amazing video of a group of tourists in a safari park who were told not to tease the animals. But the driver of their car tooted his horn at a big bull elephant which charged at them. All the man could do was drive in reverse as fast as he could. But the elephant kept coming and the people in the car were screaming. You should have heard how they panicked. Eventually, the elephant caught up with them and flipped the car over as though it was a toy."

"I've seen one even better than that," said Liz. "It was about some lions and a crocodile and a buffalo."

It turned out that everyone except the professor had **whiled away** their time in lockdown by watching animal videos on You Tube. It was a guilty secret, something they would not normally admit to anyone in public because it was so pointless although in the circumstances it was relaxing and pleasant. But now they were all laughing at themselves. It had done the trick. Their discussion about the dilemma of the lockdown had been threatening to spoil the party but now the tension was eased.

Instead of heated exchanges, there was now **friendly rivalry** between them. Who had the best story? Was it the cheetah, the elephant or the buffalo story?

Only the professor remained aloof from all the banter and the laughter. He was a serious man who liked to talk to people about serious subjects. But Liz found a way to include him in the game.

"Come on, let's have a real competition. Let's decide which is best. The professor can be the judge."

The professor, of course, was only too happy to accept the role.

So they played the videos one by one. First the one with the cheetahs, then the one with the elephants. The professor shook his head at both of them.

"What you don't seem to understand," he said, "is that these are not *animal* videos. True, they have animals in them but they are really about *people*. These are videos about *people* behaving badly. *People* doing stupid things. Not animals."

"Well, there are no people in my video," said Liz triumphantly. "Mine's just got animals of the wild kind in it."

The video was shot looking across a wide river somewhere in Africa. It opened with a herd of springboks running away from something. It was not clear at first what they were **fleeing** but the cause of their panic was soon revealed. Lions! There was a pride of lions coming along the bank but they were not after the springboks, they were chasing a big buffalo.

"Oh my god," **gasped** Maggie as the buffalo jumped into the water to escape the **pursuing** lions. It was shallow near the bank but the buffalo wanted to get as far away from the lions as possible, so it started swimming across the river. As it swam the lions – a male lion and three lionesses – prowled along the shore. Their eyes fixed firmly on the buffalo as it made its escape.

But the hunt was not over yet. The buffalo was half way across the river when a giant crocodile attacked it. Everyone

gasped this time, even Liz who had seen the video before. They **gasped** in shock and horror at what was happening.

"**Out of the frying pan and into the fire**," said the professor, as usual picking the right expression to describe the circumstances.

Meanwhile, the buffalo in a panic, turned round and started heading back to the land where the pride of lions was waiting and watching every move.

"If it makes it out, its chances of survival are practically nil," said Tony. The buffalo seemed to have had the same thought because, as soon as Tony said that, it turned around and started swimming back into the middle of the river. But the crocodile was still in **hot pursuit** and there were more **gasps** from the four friends as it launched a second attack on the buffalo.

"Oh, the poor thing," said Maggie. "I can't bear to watch."

"**It's in two minds**," said the professor. "It can't decide whether to face the crocodile or the lions."

Again, it altered course, this time swimming to the shallows where it stood panting and staring at the lions prowling on the bank while they stared back and the crocodile patrolled the river.

The standoff seemed to last forever and the four friends searched for the right words to describe what they were seeing.

"At least he's safe for the moment," said Tony.

"For the moment," agreed Maggie, "but he's still **not out of the woods**. He's still got a serious problem."

"He's **damned if he does and damned if he doesn't**," said Liz. "If he swims out into the river, the crocodile will get him. If he goes on land, the lions will get him."

"Or you could say he's between the devil and the deep blue sea," said Tony.

"Or between a rock and a hard place," said Liz.

"You are all right, of course," said the professor, "but the best word for his situation is '**dilemma**'. He's actually **on the horns of a dilemma**. Remember, the kind of problem you have when there are two courses of action open to you and they are both bad."

"You mean just like we are facing with the pandemic," said Liz. "To lock down or not to lock down, both choices will have really bad consequences."

"Precisely," said the professor. "We know what the government did. Now let's see what the buffalo does."

The buffalo stood in the shallows for what seemed like an age but must have been only a minute or two before **making up its mind** and deciding to take its chances against the lions on land even though it was **outnumbered** four to one.

The buffalo was aggressive and the lions were **wary**. They knew that they had to be careful even though the buffalo was **isolated** from its herd. The buffalo was a huge, powerful animal and if it caught a lion on its great horns, it would cause serious injury.

The lionesses formed the front line of the attack but when the buffalo lunged at them, they **backed off** and circled around him. As he moved further inland they surrounded him and the big male lion joined the hunt. When the buffalo went for the big lion, he ran away and all five animals ran along the bank. The big lion was in the lead, the buffalo chasing him followed by the three lionesses close behind.

Eventually they surrounded him again and it looked as though it would be game over. Everyone **gasped** once more.

"Oh, no!" They all said it at the same time.

"He's as good as dead," said Tony.

"Absolutely, he can't possibly survive this," said the professor.

But they spoke too soon. Help was at hand. The balance of power on the river bank suddenly changed as a great herd of buffalo came into view. The lions saw the herd coming, **turned tail** and fled. In moments the herd had taken over the river bank and the buffalo's dilemma was **resolved**. He was safe at last.

"How did that happen?" asked Tony expecting the professor, as always, to be on hand with a ready-made answer. But this time Liz was too quick for him.

"It's called herd immunity," she said.

The Vocabulary Detective

Clues in the Context

Not meant as a compliment

(5) Idiom, a chunk of language, a standard way of saying something. It is describing something so treat it as an adjective and ask: Who or what is it qualifying? And in what way, is it negative or positive?

(E) The answer to the first question is the statement that Hapgood was "the man who knows everything". The answer to the second question is that, clearly, the sense is negative and it also signals that the statement about Hapgood is about to be contradicted. In other words, "the man who knows everything" is an ironic expression and the clues that follow, all colloquial expressions or chunks of language, are details showing what people really thought of him.

> To his friends, Professor Robin Hapgood was "the man who knows everything". Even though he was a famous professor at a famous university, this was **not meant as a compliment**. Many thought he was just a know-it-all, the kind of man who loved the sound of his own voice which he used to trumpet his own opinions and drown out the ideas and views of other people.
>
> What made it worse, and even embarrassing at times for his wife and friends, was that he did not always know what he was talking about. People suspected that he sometimes just made things up so that he would sound cleverer than everyone else.

So what do you think it means?

Tender lamb

(5) Idiom, a collocation. What is special about lamb that is tender?

(D) To find the clue you have to go right back to the first paragraph where the writer conveys a similar idea in specific detail.

> As always the professor was in charge of the meat and he had cooked a rolled joint of lamb on the spit until <u>it was done to a turn, succulent and dripping with flavor</u>.
> ….
> They were as good to look at as they were to eat and formed the perfect accompaniment to the **tender lamb**.

Meaning…

Complimenting

(3) Verb. What state or action does it express? Who or what does it refer to?

(D) It refers to something that Maggie said to Liz. The clue to the meaning is in what she said.

(F) You have seen "compliment" previously in the expression "it was not meant as a compliment". Unlike the previous example of "compliment", this one was meant sincerely.

> "<u>That was so sweet</u>," said Maggie, **complimenting** Liz for her fruit salad.

Meaning…

Normality

(2) Noun. So what is it?

(C) The clue is in the form of a definition at the end of the sentence.

> The idea was that it should be a happy occasion, a relief that finally the lockdown was over and life could start moving back to some sort of **normality** and eventually everything would be like it had been before.

Meaning...

Confined

(3) Verb. What action or state does it express? And who or what does it relate to?

(D) It relates to the people at the barbecue and something that happened to them. In the next sentence you find clues in the form of specific details which should help you to get the meaning of "confined".

> And so the conversation turned to how hard it had been for everyone. They had been **confined** to their homes for six weeks in an attempt to stop the spread of the deadly pandemic. They were only allowed out to do the shopping or go to medical appointments. It was almost like being in prison, they agreed.

Meaning...

Loneliness

(2) Noun. What is it?

(D) In this context, the clue is at the end of the sentence which says in specific terms what is meant.

> The worst thing was the **loneliness**, <u>being separated from family and friends</u>.

Meaning...

Hardship

(2) Noun. What is it?

(D) The clues are specific details and examples of what is meant.

> If we shut down the economy we destroy businesses and throw lots of people out of work, causing lots of **hardship**, <u>many people won't be able to pay their rent</u> or <u>even put food on the table</u>.

Meaning...

Dilemma

(2) Noun. What is it?

(C) In this case a character in the story, Liz, asks the question for you and the answer is spelled out as a definition by the professor. This is the first of three clues.

(D) The second clue follows immediately from the definition and gives the specific detail of what makes their situation a dilemma.

> Either way there is a cost, there is a price to pay in money and lives. It is a true **dilemma**, there is no easy answer."
>
> "A what?" said Liz who had had a little bit too much to drink and hadn't really been paying much attention to the professor's lecture.

111

The Vocabulary Detective

> "A **dilemma** is a special kind of problem. <u>It's the kind of problem you have when there are two courses of action available to you and both of them are bad</u>," said the professor who was only too happy to explain. In this case the **dilemma** is clear, <u>we have a choice between saving lives and saving the economy. We can't do both.</u> As they saying goes, <u>we are caught on the horns of a dilemma.</u>"

Meaning...

Lighten up

(5) A multi word verb so ask: What action does it express? And who does it refer to? The answer to these questions is that it is something that Maggie wants the others to do.

(D) The clues to the meaning follow immediately in the form of a series of details and examples of exactly what she means by "lighten up".

(E) And finally there is a contrast for emphasis between "light", "amusing" and "entertaining" on the one hand and "gloomy" on the other.

> Can't we just **lighten up** a little? Can't we talk about something <u>less depressing</u>? Something <u>light</u>, something <u>amusing</u>, something <u>entertaining</u>. Something that's <u>not so damn gloomy</u>."

Meaning...

Contempt

(2) Noun. So ask: What is it?

(D) The clues are in the next sentence which says specifically what the professor thought.

> Everyone laughed except the professor who had nothing but **contempt** for You Tube animal videos. <u>To him, they were trivial and a complete waste of time</u>.

Meaning…

Whiled away

(5) A multi-word verb so ask: What action or state does it express and who does it refer to? The answer is that it referred to Maggie, Liz and Tony and expressed something they had done during the lockdown.

(D) The details and specific examples that follow are good clues to the meaning. The first detail tells you exactly what they did and the second gives you an idea how they felt when doing it.

> It turned out that everyone except the professor had **whiled away** their time in lockdown by <u>watching animal videos on You Tube</u>. It was a guilty secret, something they would not normally admit to anyone in public because it was so pointless although in the circumstances it was <u>relaxing and pleasant</u>.

Meaning…

Friendly rivalry

(5) Idiom, a collocation. Ask: What is rivalry? And how does the adjective "friendly" modify the meaning?

(D) In the next sentence you find a clue to the first question. Rivalry is to do with competition.

The Vocabulary Detective

(E) In the previous sentence, there is a contrast. Instead of "heated exchanges", which suggests anger, you have something between friends.

(F) You might also recall that in *The Lucky Number Fourteen*, "rivalry" was used in a different context and it was certainly not "friendly".

> Instead of <u>heated exchanges,</u> there was now **friendly rivalry** between them. <u>Who had the best story</u>?

Meaning...

Fleeing

(3) Verb. So ask: What state or action does it express? Who or what does it refer to?

(B) It refers to the springboks and the clue is in the previous sentence. "Fleeing" is a synonym for the multi-word verb "running away from".

(F) This verb is also used in the story *The Lucky Number Fourteen*.

> The video was shot looking across a wide river somewhere in Africa. It opened with a herd of springboks <u>running away from</u> something. It was not clear at first what they were **fleeing** but the cause of their panic was soon revealed.

Meaning...

Pursuing

(3) Adjective. What word does it qualify and in what way?

(B) It refers to the lions. The clue to the meaning is in the previous sentence which explains what the lions were doing.

The Buffalo's Dilemma

There was a pride of lions coming along the bank but they were not after the springboks, they were <u>chasing</u> a big buffalo.

"Oh my god," gasped Maggie as the buffalo jumped into the water to escape the **pursuing** lions.

Meaning…

Gasped

(3) Verb. So ask: What state or action does it express? Who or what does it refer to?

(D) When this verb is used for the first time it refers to Maggie and this points to two clues: what Maggie said and the specific detail of what she was reacting to.

(F) The word is used twice more in the next paragraph which should help you to get an idea of what it means. In this paragraph it refers to everyone, not just Maggie, and again it gives specific detail of what they were reacting to plus a description of the way they reacted.

"<u>Oh my god</u>," **gasped** Maggie <u>as the buffalo jumped into the water to escape the pursuing lions</u>. It was shallow near the bank but the buffalo wanted to get as far away from the lions as possible, so it started swimming across the river. As it swam the lions – a male lion and three lionesses – prowled along the shore. Their eyes fixed firmly on the buffalo as it made its escape.

But the hunt was not over yet. <u>The buffalo was half way across the river when a giant crocodile attacked it</u>. Everyone **gasped**

115

this time, even Liz who had seen the video before. They **gasped** in shock and horror at what was happening.
Meaning…

Out of the frying pan and into the fire

(5) Idiom, a colloquial expression but there is no frying pan or fire in this story, so ask: Exactly what is this referring to?

(D) As the text says, the expression refers to the circumstances of the buffalo, having escaped the lions on land (out of the frying pan) it was now facing danger from the crocodile in the river (into the fire).

> "**Out of the frying pan and into the fire**," said the professor, as usual picking the right expression to describe the circumstances.

Meaning…

Hot pursuit

(5) Idiom. "Hot pursuit" is a collocation made up of a noun and an adjective. Ask about the noun first: What is a "pursuit"?

(A) First look closely at the word "pursuit" and you might notice that it is the noun form of the verb "pursue" which you have already seen in the story.

(D) Then look more widely for clues and you will see specific details that should help you to imagine the scene. Next, you need to ask: In what way does the adjective "hot" modify the noun? More specifically, do you think the crocodile was swimming slowly or do you think it was in a hurry?

> The buffalo seemed to have had the same thought because, as soon as Tony said that, it turned around and started swimming back

into the middle of the river. But the crocodile was still in **hot pursuit** and there were more gasps from the four friends as it launched a second attack on the buffalo.

Meaning…

Gasps

(F) The meaning is repeated using a noun instead of a verb so ask: What caused the **gasps** this time? Or what caused them **to gasp** this time?

>…there were more **gasps** from the four friends as it launched a second attack on the buffalo.

Meaning…

In two minds

(5) Colloquial expression. Who or what is in two minds and why?

(B) The buffalo is in two minds and the professor gives a good clue to the meaning when he says "it can't decide" which is synonymous with being "in two minds".

>"**It's in two minds**," said the professor.
>"It can't decide whether to face the crocodile or the lions."

(D) To help you clarify the meaning, look at the following sentence which gives a specific description of the buffalo and shows that it could not decide what to do.

>Again, it altered course, this time swimming to the shallows where it stood

panting and staring at the lions prowling on the bank while they stared back and the crocodile patrolled the river.

Meaning...

Not out of the woods

(5) Colloquial expression which has nothing to do with "woods". So what does it refer to?

(C) Maggie gives a clue when she repeats the idea with what is, effectively, a definition of what she means.

> "At least he's safe for the moment," said Tony.
> "For the moment," agreed Maggie, "but he's still **not out of the woods**. He's still got a serious problem."

Meaning...

Damned if he does and damned if he doesn't

(5) Colloquial expression. So ask: What is his position exactly?

(D) Liz gives the specific details that should make the meaning clear.

> "He's **damned if he does and damned if he doesn't**," said Liz. "If he swims out into the river, the crocodile will get him. If he goes on land, the lions will get him."

(B) Tony and Liz give other colloquial expressions with similar meanings.

> "Or you could say he's between the devil and the deep blue sea," said Tony.

"Or between a rock and a hard place," said Liz.

Meaning...

On the horns of a dilemma

(5) Colloquial expression. Ask: What does it mean to be "on the horns of a dilemma"?

(C) The professor provides a definition.

(F) Note this idea is repeated, it's the central focus of the story and is in the title as well.

> "You are all right, of course," said the professor, "but the best word for his situation is '**dilemma**'. He's actually **on the horns of a dilemma**. Remember, the kind of problem you have when there are two courses of action open to you and they are both bad."
>
> "You mean just like we are facing with the pandemic," said Liz. "To lock down or not to lock down, both choices will have really bad consequences."

Meaning...

Making up its mind

(5) Colloquial expression. So what did it do?

(B) The expression is followed by a synonym that should give you the meaning.

(F) Note that this is related to the expression "in two minds" above.

> The buffalo stood in the shallows for what seemed like an age but must have been only a minute or two before **making up its**

mind and <u>deciding</u> to take its chances against the lions on land even though it was outnumbered four to one.

Meaning...

Outnumbered

(3) Verb. What action or state does it express? And who or what does it refer to?

(A) Before answering those questions look at the word itself, which is made up of "numbered" and the prefix "out" which usually means "more than". You might be able to pick the meaning from this.

(D) Then answer the questions. Clearly the word refers to the buffalo and this directs you to the main clue which is the specific detail.

> The buffalo stood in the shallows for what seemed like an age but must have been only a minute or two before making up its mind and deciding to take its chances against the lions on land even though it was **outnumbered** <u>four to one</u>.

Meaning...

Wary

(4) Adjective. What word does it qualify? And in what way?

(B) It qualifies "the lions" and in the next sentence the synonym "careful" should help you answer the second question.

(D) So why did it need to be careful? In the next sentences there are details that answer this question and should help you clarify the meaning of "wary".

The Buffalo's Dilemma

> The buffalo was aggressive and the lions were **wary**. They knew that they had to be <u>careful</u> even though the buffalo was isolated from its herd. The buffalo was a huge, powerful animal and <u>if it caught a lion on its great horns, it would cause serious injury</u>.

Meaning…

Isolated

(3) Verb. What state or action does it express? And who or what does it refer to?

(D) It refers to the buffalo and a clue to the meaning comes in the form of a specific detail following the word "isolated".

> The buffalo was aggressive and the lions were wary. They knew that they had to be careful even though the buffalo was **isolated** <u>from its herd</u>.

Meaning…

Backed off

(5) Idiom, a multi-word verb so ask: What action or state does it express? And who or what does it refer to?

(E) The clue is a contrast. The buffalo "lunged at them" meaning it moved aggressively towards them, so they did the opposite.

> The lionesses formed the front line of the attack <u>but when the buffalo lunged at them</u>, they **backed off** and circled around him.

Meaning…

121

Gasped

(F) Repeated word.

> Eventually <u>they surrounded him again</u> and <u>it looked as though it would be game over</u>. Everyone **gasped** once more.

Meaning...

Turned tail

(5) Colloquial expression. As it expresses an action ask: What action? And who or what does it relate to?

(C) It refers to the lions and the clue to the meaning is the verb "fled" which is the past tense of the verb "flee". We have already seen the present participle used. So what happens just before one animal runs away from another?

> The lions saw the herd coming, **turned tail** and <u>fled</u>.

Meaning...

Resolved

(3) Verb. So ask: What state or action does it express? And who or what does it refer to?

(D) It refers to the "buffalo's dilemma". In the next sentence is the specific detail that explains how it was "resolved".

> In moments the herd had taken over the river bank and the buffalo's dilemma was **resolved**. He was <u>safe at last</u>.

Meaning...

About the author

David Hastings has spent his entire professional life working with the English language as a journalist, author and teacher. His journalism career included roles as reporter, television news producer and newspaper editor. He has also written four widely praised non-fiction books. *Over the Mountains of the Sea*, which describes what it was like on the migration voyage to New Zealand in the age of sail; *Extra! Extra! How the people made the news*, a history of newspapers; *The Many Deaths of Mary Dobie*, the story of a murder and its aftermath; and *Odyssey of the Unknown Anzac* which is a biography of a man caught between the horror of war and a terrifying mental illness.

Over the Mountains of the Sea
    The nautical experiences of these migrants … are presented in absorbing detail in Hastings' book.
    Kennedy Warne, New Zealand Geographic

    Hastings … has a journalist's eye for a good story and a historian's determination to work out what the stories mean.
    Deborah Montgomerie, New Zealand Books

This is a very entertaining and user-friendly tale, or tales, written with a journalist's eye for the curious and bizarre as well as the broader detail.
Mick Ludden, Wairarapa Times-Age

Hastings ... demonstrates that the journey was even more stressful than we suspected, testing even for people used to a level of hardship that we have trouble imagining.
Gordon McLauchlan, New Zealand Herald

Extra! Extra! How the people made the news
This look at Auckland's early newspapers mixes entertaining anecdotes with bigger philosophies.
Kevin Childs, The Walkley Magazine

Extra! Extra! How the People Made the News covers the turbulent fortunes of Auckland's newspapers over six decades, from the 1840s to the turn of the century ... the book gives an illuminating and well-rounded history of the papers, their place in the community and country and their unending efforts to attract and retain readers.
Michael Potts, Media International Australia

An excellent book that seamlessly combines scholarship with a feel for the dynamics of newsgathering and the reading public's insatiable curiosity about human frailty.
Ian F. Grant, Journal of New Zealand Studies, 2013

The Many Deaths of Mary Dobie
This is not a thriller or a whodunnit: indeed it is meticulously researched, thoughtful, unshowy and compassionate. It is compulsive reading nonetheless.
William Brandt, New Zealand Books, Winter 2016

It's a book that I, as a public historian, really find quite exciting …. A sophisticated retelling of New Zealand history, trying to understand what happened from different perspectives.
Paul Diamond, Radio New Zealand, Nine to Noon

Odyssey of the Unknown Anzac
Behind every name on the rows of headstones in New Zealand servicemen's cemeteries … is a story to be told. This is one such story, told by a writer whose lifetime in journalism ensures it has been told with attention to detail and great humanity.
Jim Sullivan, Otago Daily Times

A new and fascinating work of history … Hastings proceeds to reconstruct McQuay's war and journey to the mental hospital. This is not an easy task. There is no memoir, no letters, even the army record is deficient. Hastings manages to do so through a brilliant use of sources.
Jock Phillips, New Zealand Review of Books

Odyssey of the Unknown Anzac draws the reader's thoughts towards aspects of the war experience – post-traumatic stress, disability and mental illness – that sit awkwardly with commemorative myths of returned heroes and the glorious dead.
Samuel Finnemore, New Zealand Listener

Printed in Great Britain
by Amazon